MW00637872

LEATHER CRAFTING STARTER BOOK

Tools, Techniques, and 16 Step-by-Step Projects for Beginners

STUDIO TAC CREATIVE, IN PARTNERSHIP WITH CRAFT & CO., LTD.

FOX CHAPEL
PUBLISHING

Throughout, projects were made using Japanese tools that have different measurements. When recreating these projects, sizes (especially sizes of holes made with instruments) may be slightly different due to the availability of tools in your region. An approximation has been made, based on standard tool sizes found in North America and the UK.

LEATHER CRAFTING STARTER BOOK
Copyright ©2012 STUDIO TAC CREATIVE CO., LTD.
All rights reserved.
Original Japanese edition published by STUDIO TAC CREATIVE CO.,LTD. Photographer: Hideyo Komine, Takashi Sakamoto, Tomonari Sasaki, Masato Shibata
This English language edition is published by arrangement with STUDIO TAC CREATIVE CO., LTD.
English translation rights ©2019 by FOX CHAPEL PUBLISHING, 903 Square Street, Mount Joy, PA 17552.

The patterns contained herein are copyrighted by the author. Readers may make copies of these patterns for personal use. The patterns themselves, however, are not to be duplicated for resale or distribution under any circumstances. Any such copying is a violation of copyright law.

ISBN 978-1-56523-952-4

Library of Congress Cataloging-in-Publication Data

Names: Sutajio Takku Kurieitivu, author.
Title: Leather crafting starter book / Studio Tac Creative.
Other titles: Rezåa kurafuto sutåato bukku. English
Description: English language edition. I Mount Joy : Fox Chapel Publishing,
    [2018] I In English, translated from Japanese. I Translation of: Rezåa
    kurafuto sutåato bukku. I Includes index.
Identifiers: LCCN 2018048028 (print) I LCCN 2018049219 (ebook) I ISBN
    9781607655428 (ebook) I ISBN 9781565239524 (softcover)
Subjects: LCSH: Leatherwork.
Classification: LCC TT290 (ebook) I LCC TT290 .R4613 2018 (print) I DDC
    745.53/1--dc23
LC record available at https://lccn.loc.gov/2018048028

To learn more about the other great books from Fox Chapel Publishing, or to find a retailer near you, call toll-free 1-800-457-9112 or visit us at *www.FoxChapelPublishing.com*.

We are always looking for talented authors. To submit an idea, please send a brief inquiry to acquisitions@foxchapelpublishing.com.

Printed in Singapore
First printing

Because working with leather and other materials inherently includes the risk of injury and damage, this book cannot guarantee that creating the projects in this book is safe for everyone. For this reason, this book is sold without warranties or guarantees of any kind, expressed or implied, and the publisher and the author disclaim any liability for any injuries, losses, or damages caused in any way by the content of this book or the reader's use of the tools needed to complete the projects presented here. The publisher and the author urge all readers to thoroughly review each project and to understand the use of all tools before beginning any project.

Contents

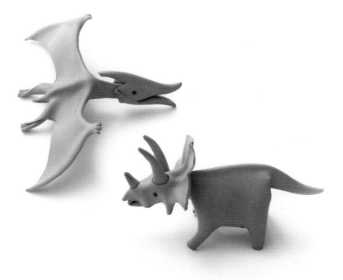

CRAFT & CO., LTD.: PRODUCER OF ALL THE LEATHER USED IN THIS BOOK'S PROJECTS

At walking distance from Tokyo's JR Ogikubo station, Craft & Co., Ltd., is the only store in Japan that specializes in leather crafting. It is not an exaggeration to say that you can find anything you need for this craft in this store. You will find a large shop floor that stores both popular and more peculiar tools and materials. The staff here are knowledgeable and can help you go through your project.

You will be able to find anything you need on this large shop floor. If you are lost, just ask the staff for some advice.

SHOP DATA
Craft & Co., Ltd.
Ogikubo 5-16-15
Suginamiku, Tokyo
Open 11:00 AM–7:00 PM (2nd & 4th Sat:
10:00 AM–6:00 PM)
Closed on Sun; 1st, 3rd & 5th Sat;
and Festivities
http://www.craftsha.co.jp

1. Vegetable-tanned leather, chrome-tanned leather, etc. There are many types of leather from which to choose. 2. The majority of the tools come from the store's line of products, but you can also find non-Japanese brands. 3. This leather is from Craft & Co.'s own brand, which comes in different thicknesses and treatments. 4. There are also special types of leather which have been treated with foil, etc. 5. There is more leather stored at the back of the shop!

Also offered is a substantial curriculum that gives lessons to both beginners and those with experience. Since there are also a correspondence course and a summer course, a lecture can be taken at the learner's convenience.

The seminars and workshops offered are tailored to the needs and pace of each student.

AN INTRODUCTION TO

Leather Crafting

"Leather crafting is so difficult." That's something we hear a lot from people who never tried leather crafting. Yes, it's true; you will not be able to make leather bags and leather shoes without some practice, but if we are talking about small accessories, there are plenty of projects that you can start right away, without any previous experience in the craft.

This book covers the basics of leather crafting, but it also goes into more advanced projects that you can make with a small leather crafting kit. All you need is to get started with something you feel like making.

Few are the people who have mastered leather crafting, yet there are many ways to get into this craft.

The reason you are holding this book in your hands is probably because you have some interest in leather working. So why not give it a shot?

Basic Techniques 19

In this section, you will find the basic leather crafting techniques explained. For those who have never tried this craft before, try reading this part first and practice a little before starting your projects. Once done, you will be able to make a smooth start in the art of leather crafting.

Decorative Techniques 45

As shown here, decorative techniques can considerably broaden the art of leather crafting. It's easy to add a touch of originality by just slightly altering the design of your item.

Step 1

No-Sew Items 57

The accessories in this section require only some polishing and gluing. You will not have to stitch or use a lot of tools. These little projects are thus a good starting point to learn more about leather's peculiar characteristics, as well as its handling and processing. Let's get started with the ABCs of leather making!

Step 2

Basic Stitching 105

These items can be made with basic hand stitching, darning, and machine sewing methods. You might find it difficult to sew at first, but as you get the hang of it, sewing too will become easy. You can also start customizing our patterns and enjoy the results.

Step 3

Complex Designs 143

This is an introduction to creating more complicated items. Because there are more parts to put together and more layered sewing to be done, you will need more time to craft these items. But as we are still using basic techniques, these projects are still accessible to beginners.

Unisex

Here is a collection of items that could easily suit anyone. They will make a great handmade gift to yourself or your loved ones.

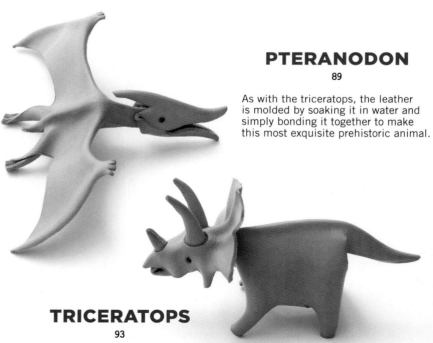

PTERANODON
89

As with the triceratops, the leather is molded by soaking it in water and simply bonding it together to make this most exquisite prehistoric animal.

TRICERATOPS
93

This dinosaur figure can be made by using moisture and pasting it together with a bond. Such a three-dimensional item is characteristic of the versatility of leather.

PEN COVER
112

This is a pen cover that you can use with a cheap pen to add a level of refinement to it. With time, the leather will take the shape of your hand, making it easier for you to write with it.

8

PEN CASE
122

The stiffness and longer cover flap of the case are designed to provide better protection for your pens. You can also personalize it by changing the color of the belt and the thread.

KEY COVER
108

With a little bit of fiddling, you can transform your key into an elegant accessory. As it requires very little stitching, this is the perfect project for those who want to practice sewing. Why not try creating them in different colors?

BABOUCHES
152

These are double-stitched babouches. They are easier to make than it looks, and you cannot go wrong if you cut the leather according to the paper pattern!

DESK TRAY
82

By using the technique of "stacked leather"— pieces of leather piled one on top of the other— you can create this minimal-looking tray. You just need to really polish the edges of the stacked leather to get a smooth, finished look.

Men's

More rugged in style, these leather items are more masculine. Why not craft them with thicker leather? You will be able to witness the patina changing beautifully as the leather ages. We recommend you use unbleached leather for these items.

BUSINESS CARD HOLDER

116

A one-of-a-kind card holder that will help distinguish you from the rest. Easy to customize, you can play with the colors of the leather string and the shape of the button.

BRACELET

64

Comfortable and easy to wear, this bracelet is very easy to create. You just need to cut the leather according to the paper pattern, polish it, apply the stud closure, and you are done! Then just wear it all the time, allowing water, sun, and your skin to patina the leather.

SHEEP SKULL NECKLACE

98

Resembles the real thing. We have researched the best way to create a texture that would look and feel like a sheep skull. The necklace is further embellished with leather beads.

WALLET CORD

76

This cord can easily be made without any tools by simply braiding it. Make it in the same color as your wallet.

MEDIUM-SIZED WALLET

144

With many parts to assemble, this is a fun project that will give you an easy-to-use, long-lasting, handmade wallet.

ENGRAVED BRACELET

67

By carving a pattern on it, you will create a unique bracelet. Draw your own design for a distinctly original item!

Women's

This is a collection of feminine and modern items for everyday life. Even without any knowledge of leather crafting, it is easy to enjoy these projects by selecting your own colors and designs.

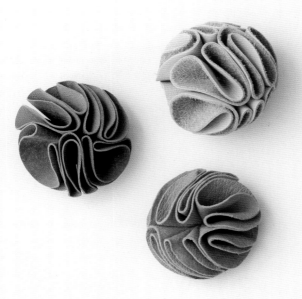

POM-POM CHARM
71

Slightly unusual in shape, they can be made without any stitching. They are easy to combine with other accessories and are a perfect little gift.

CARD HOLDER
130

A cute and handy card holder created with a running stitch. We opened two round holes so that you know which card is in the card holder.

12

FLOWER CHARM
73

Making use of the characteristics of chrome-tanned leather, we were able to create these full-bodied flowers. They can easily be pinned to your blazer or in your hair. These only require glue to make them.

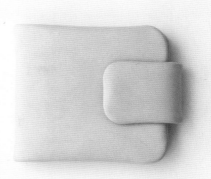

BIFOLD WALLET
158

Soft to the touch, thanks to the sponge inserted on the inside, this wallet is also very practical as it has a very large capacity.

TASSELS
60

These are delicate accessories that will add class to your style. Just have fun combining and varying the colors and size of these tassels!

TOTE BAG
136

A bag that is perfect for more casual outings, it can easily be created if you have a sewing machine that can handle leather.

The Basic Tools and Materials for Leather Crafting

You will be able to get through most of this book with only a basic leather crafting toolbox, a standard hand sewing kit, and round drive punch tools. With these, you will be able to create leatherware of a high standard. The latter is used to open clean-cut holes and comes in more than 20 different sizes.

If you plan to increase the quality and complexity of your crafts, you will need to buy more tools. Owning and using new tools can be another pleasure of leather crafting.

GETTING A STARTER KIT

You can buy each tool individually, but that can quickly get expensive and complicated. Instead, buying a starter kit will get you the basics.

WHAT A BASIC LEATHER CRAFTING TOOLBOX MIGHT CONTAIN

Japanese leather knife
A Japanese-style leather knife. The blade is exchangeable.

Plastic bone folder, creaser, or slicker
To crease, slick, and fold leather. Also used to polish the flesh side and cut edges of leather.

Thonging chisel
To punch the holes before you sew them. You can do most projects with a set of two- and four-pronged chisels.

Round awl
To mark the position of stitches and patterns on the leather. Also used to apply glue.

Wooden mallet (medium)
To punch holes or drive stamps into the leather, as well as for flattening stitches.

Glue applicator stick
Made of plastic, its shape makes it easy to apply glue in a thin and uniform way for all of your projects.

Sewing needle (blunt and fine)
The basic type of needle for hand-sewing leather craft.

Beeswax
Slide your thread over the wax to thinly coat it and make it stronger and smoother.

Natural linen thread (medium)
A basic thread made of linen. Used after you have waxed it.

Sanding stick
To sand uneven edges or to smooth out the leather after it has been beveled. Also used to rasp the leather before applying glue.

Edge beveler (no.1)
Bevels and rounds off edges. No.1's blade has a width of 0.8mm.

Adjustable stitching groover
Makes a clean groove on thick leather to facilitate stitching. The blade can easily be adjusted.

Flex glue
Water-based adhesive that is white when applied and dries clear and flexible. Nontoxic, with very little smell. Apply to both sides and bond before it dries.

Glossing polish
To polish vegetable-tanned leather. If applied over the cut edges and flesh side before polishing, it will smooth fuzzy leather.

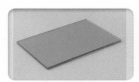

PVC cutting mat
To be used when cutting and shaping leather. The PVC will prevent the blade from being damaged.

Rubber mat
To use with thonging chisels, the drive punch, and other tools that need to be driven into the leather. The rubber will preserve the tip of the tools.

Felt mat
Used under the rubber mat, it helps absorb noises.

TO BE BOUGHT SEPARATELY IF NOT INCLUDED:

Leather round drive punch tool
To drive round holes into the leather before applying any metal fittings. To be used on the rubber mat.

Instruction booklet on hand-sewing leather
The foundations of hand-sewing leather craft are indicated.

One or a few starter's kits
Great to practice on before starting your own projects.

Four Points to Know

For those of you who are just starting with the craft, you should be aware of the four fundamentals of leather craft. In this book, you will find the instructions and the paper patterns that go along with each project. If you follow them through, you will be able to finish the project. However, there are four points on the properties of leather you ought to know if you want your accessories to be durable, easy to use, and of high quality. Once you have these simple points in mind, you will be able to appreciate more the process of crafting leather.

1 LEATHER TANNING

When you consider the type of leather to use in your projects, you will need to pay close attention to three things: its "elasticity," "thickness," and "tanning." The texture and elasticity of the leather are largely determined by the type of tanning used on the leather. On the right are the most common methods of tanning and their properties.

Throughout, we list the type of leather recommended for each project. In order to choose the best material, just remember these points, go to a leather craft store, and feel with your hands the different types of hide available.

Vegetable tanning (tannin)
Vegetable-tanned hide is resistant and flexible. It will absorb the traces of our daily life and develop a warm patina over the years. Both the grain and flesh sides can be polished.

Chrome tanning
More supple, pliable, and resilient than vegetable-tanned leather. It can have the texture of skin and is widely used to make jackets, bags, and other accessories.

Combination tanned
Tanned with two or more agents. You could, for instance, have an initial chrome tanning and then a vegetable retanning. It allows the leather to take the characteristics of both tanning methods.

Vegetable-tanned leather: natural aging
Over the years, the leather will acquire a warmer and more brilliant shade, giving leather its vintage, unique character.

Chrome-tanned leather: soft to the touch
Chrome gives elasticity and softness to the items. It is indispensible for accessories that require sewing on the inside.

2 GRAIN SIDE & FLESH SIDE

The grain side of the leather is the outer layer of the animal skin that has been de-haired. The flesh side is the hide that was next to the flesh. Normally, the grain side will appear on the outside and flesh side will be used on the lining. If the flesh side is to be seen, you will have to polish it with an agent.

Grain Flesh

The difference between the two sides is quite obvious: While the grain side is smooth, the flesh side is tight and slightly "fuzzy." As the cut edges present the same properties as the flesh side, it will be necessary to polish them if you want to show them.

3 LEATHER HIDE SUBDIVISION

As a hide comes from an animal skin, the elasticity of the leather will depend on the flow of the grain. The leather will stretch better if you follow the direction of the grain, while it will be firmer and stronger perpendicular to the grain flow. It is thus good practice to notice how the grain flows when working with leather. The top right image illustrates the right half or "side" of a cowhide. The side can be subdivided into different cuts, each having a different level of elasticity. The easiest cut to work on is the single bend, where the grain flows in only one direction.

You can also check the direction of the grain flow by touching and bending the leather with your hands.

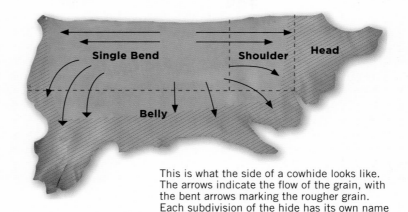

This is what the side of a cowhide looks like. The arrows indicate the flow of the grain, with the bent arrows marking the rougher grain. Each subdivision of the hide has its own name with its own characteristics.

Choosing your leather section

(A) Like this card holder, some items are folded when used. The crease and the grain flow will have to run in the same direction. (B) To prevent pockets from stretching over time, make sure that the grain flow is parallel to the opening. (C) Cut along the flow of the grain to better retain the shapes of items that should not be stretched.

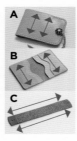

It is possible to understand the flow of the grain by folding, bending, and stretching the leather in different directions with your hands.

4 PURCHASING LEATHER

When buying leather, keep in mind the above-mentioned points. The elasticity, thickness, and tanning methods will all depend on the type of item you want to create. Ideally, you will want to go to a leather craft shop and personally choose the type and quality of the leather you will buy. But you can always ask the salesperson for advice.

The leather craft shop will have a variety of hides in stock. When buying, make sure that the texture and thickness of the leather are right for your project. Please be careful not to stain the leather when handling it.

Leather thinning services

Leather hides can come in different thicknesses. If you have set your heart on a particular hide that is too thick, you can ask your store for their leather thinning services, where the leather's edges will be pared to reduce its thickness.

Usually the hide is cut into two halves, or "sides," but there might be other types of cut. It is not always possible to get hold of the desired cut, thickness, and type of leather. In those cases, make the most out of what you will be able to purchase.

Workflow Chart

STEP 1

Choosing

First of all, choose the design and characteristics of the item you want to make. Try to be as precise as possible. Then, depending on the sewing method (machine or hand-sewn), choose the type of leather hide you will use.

For beginners, try to pick one item in the book. The sewing method, type of leather, and materials needed will be listed for each accessory.

STEP 2

Cutting

With the paper pattern, measure and mark the area to be cut on the leather. With a sharp blade, cut it on a flat surface. We recommend you practice cutting straight and curved lines on scraps of leather.

With leather, it is always possible to trim or hide the excess leather in the linings. But to save time, try to cut the leather as cleanly and close to the paper pattern as possible.

STEP 3

Sewing

With glue, fix the parts together and sew or cross-stitch them by hand or by machine. For more complicated items, pay attention to the right order, whether parts are to be glued or to be sewed.

Being able to see how a piece of flat leather is gradually transformed into something unique and handmade is one of the joys of crafting.

STEP 4

Finishing Off

The cut edges of the leather (especially vegetable-tanned leather) will greatly influence the look of the object. To increase the quality of the item, polish the edges and bring the shine out.

You can use tools like an edge beveler or a sanding stick to trim off the edges in excess, and polish the leather with some glossing polish. Please be aware that some items will require you to trim and polish the leather throughout the project.

Basic Techniques

The beginner leather crafter should first master the techniques introduced here.

Hand-Sewing: The Basics

Stitching by hand is one of the most important skills there is to know in leather crafting. Here we will show you the most basic methods in hand-stitching. Once you have mastered these, you will be able to do any of the projects in this book, even those usually done by machine. You can change the color and types of thread, as well as the width between the prongs of the thonging chisel, to get different results!

TRACING PATTERNS ONTO LEATHER

One of the first steps in leather crafting will be transferring the paper pattern to the leather. With vegetable-tanned leather, this should be done on the grain side with a round awl.

THINGS YOU'LL NEED

Round Awl
Used to transfer the pattern to the leather. For chrome leather, use a silver pen.

1 You should paste or copy your pattern onto a thicker paper, then cut it. When copying it, do it as precisely as possible, otherwise you will end up with non-matching pieces of leather.

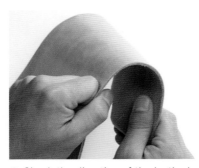

2 Check the direction of the leather's grain flow, especially for items that need to be folded.

3 Trace the pattern onto the grain side of the leather with a round awl. Hold your awl like a pen, slanted, to avoid poking through the paper.

4 Check the pattern. You should be able to see a lighter indent on the leather.

5 If you need to transfer points, poke the pattern and the leather by holding your awl vertically.

6 We have just transferred the pattern and the cardinal points onto the leather.

CUTTING LEATHER

You can use any tool that you think would be suitable, but in this case we will use the leather knife, which can be found in a basic leather craft toolbox.

THINGS YOU'LL NEED

Leather knife
Used to cut the leather.

Vinyl mat
Without it, you'd have trouble cutting the leather.

1 This is the correct way of holding a leather knife. You will have to slightly slant the blade toward the outside and the front to get a better grip for your blade.

2 When making a straight cut, do it with a sweeping and large movement.

3 At the end of your cut, bring your blade down like in the picture.

4 When cutting a disc or curve, keep your blade slanted, and for a better result move the leather instead of the knife.

5 You've now cut all your parts out. Double-check that you have not forgotten anything.

TREATING THE FLESH SIDE

Unless the flesh side is in the linings, you will need to apply a finish on the flesh side of vegetable-tanned leather to buff it and give it a more professional look.

THINGS YOU'LL NEED

Glossing polish
Used to buff the edges and flesh side of leather to "seal" it.

Plastic bone folder
Used to burnish the edges and flesh after you've applied the finish. It has other purposes, too.

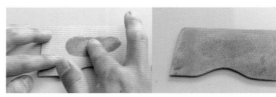

1 Apply the polish directly with your fingers and spread it on the whole surface. Don't spill it on the grain side, or you will end up with a nasty stain.

2 Before the product dries, rub the flesh with the bone folder until it is well buffed.

TIP

For larger surfaces, you can become more efficient by using a glass trowel (sold in craft stores).

TREATING THE EDGES

The edges of vegetable-tanned leather need to be buffed for a more professional look. Follow the instructions of your project, as some edges need to be finished before being sewn and others after sewing. If your leather is thin, just sand it down.

THINGS YOU'LL NEED

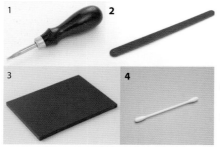

1. Edge beveler smoothes edges; 2. Sanding stick has an abrasive surface; 3. PVC mat is used as a support; 4. Cotton swab is great for applying finish to the edges.

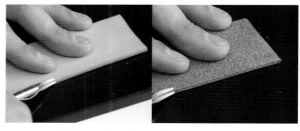

1 Round off the angles of both flesh and grain sides with the edge beveler. The standard blades are ½2" (0.8mm) and 1⁄16" (1mm). Use depending on the thickness of the leather.

2 File the edges with the sanding stick to make them rounder.

3 Apply the polish with the cotton swab. Don't spill on the grain side.

4 Rub with the bone folder. Usually, you will start from the angle on the flesh side and rub the curve until you reach the grain side.

5 Using the edge slicker on the bone folder, slick the edges with horizontal movements. For thinner leather, use the bone folder itself.

6 With a little elbow grease, vigorously polish the edges with a thick cloth.

TIP

A wood trowel is a wooden tool used to burnish leather. It is easy to use and great for reaching small areas that are often hard to polish.

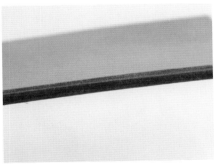

7 A finished edge should look like this. The fuzziness of the flesh will have given way to a smooth and shiny surface.

8 Before sewing the leather together, pause and think about the edges that need to be finished beforehand.

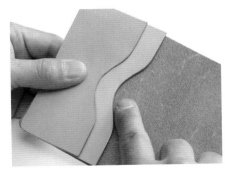

9 For instance, this card case's opening needs to be burnished before we start stitching.

10 As you can see, you won't be able to polish the opening after you have stitched the card case together.

GLUING THE LEATHER TOGETHER

You will have to wait for the flex glue to dry before you can glue the parts together, but you can always reposition the pieces after they have been glued. You cannot do this with gum-type glues. Try to spread adhesives and cements as thinly as possible.

THINGS YOU'LL NEED

Glue applicator sticks
Available in different sizes, this is the easiest way to apply adhesives and cements to your projects.

Flex glue
Water-based adhesive that is white when applied and dries clear and flexible. Nontoxic, with very little smell. Apply to both sides and bond before it dries.

Super glue
Fast-setting, strong bond adhesive. Surfaces need to be bonded before glue dries. The glue contains solvent, so ventilate your workshop when using it.

Rubber cement
Weaker, temporary glue: parts can be repositioned and glue can be peeled off. Apply to both sides, let dry until tacky, and press parts together.

Contact cement
A strong permanent glue. Apply to both sides, leave to dry, and press parts together. This is either water-based or solvent-based. When using the solvent base, ventilate your workshop.

1 Lightly trace the areas that need to be glued with a round awl. This is usually a ⅛" (3mm)-margin stitching area.

2 File these areas with a sanding stick.

3 The area should now be lighter in color. If you finish off the edges now, the glue might peel later.

4 In the case of a stitching area, apply a thin coat of glue on a ⅛" (3mm) margin. If you are using flex glue, try to do your work quickly before the glue dries.

5 Place the two pieces together and press.

6 Rub the glued parts with a bone folder.

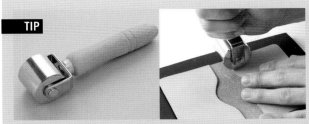

TIP

You can also use a roller, but take care not to damage the leather with this tool.

7 When gluing the grain side, follow the same steps, and sand down the area too.

8 Then apply flex glue and press together. If you don't sand down the grain, you will see the glue coming off the leather.

9 Once it's dry, file the unevenness of the edges.

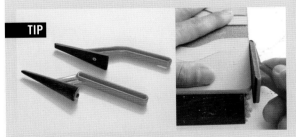

TIP

You can use a sanding pad with a handle to be more efficient.

TIP

With a smoothing plane, you can smooth out many layers of leather at the same time!

Choosing your adhesive

The adhesive included in your starter kit is strong and can be used in most of the projects. But there are other alternatives. When you need something softer, use a rubber cement. For metallic parts and other materials, use a stronger adhesive, such as super glue. For machine-sewing, use flex glue. Your work will be smoother.

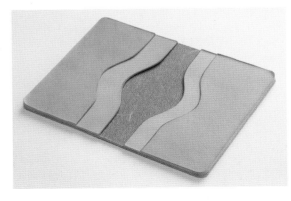

10 You are done once you finished adjusting the edges of your piece.

OPENING YOUR STITCHING SLITS

When hand-sewing, you will need to open your holes with a thonging chisel. You will achieve different looks with different sizes of chisel.

▶ **Edge creasing**

THINGS YOU'LL NEED

Plastic bone folder
You can create a stitching groove by using the slicking device on top of the bone folder.

Compass
There are other ways to get around this, but it is a useful tool to crease with.

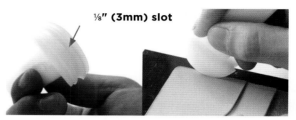

⅛" (3mm) slot

1 Trace the stitching crease using the ⅛" (3mm)-wide edge trowel. Use on both sides on leather that is thinner than ²⁄₃₂" (1.5mm).

2 For leather thicker than ¹⁄₁₆" (1.6mm), use an adjustable stitching groover. Adjust the space between the edge and the groove with the screw.

3 Place it on the leather with the center post against the edge of the leather, adjust its slant, and pull it toward you to get a stitching groove. The depth of the groove will change depending on the angle of your groover.

▶ **Opening stitching holes**

THINGS YOU'LL NEED

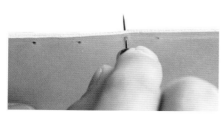

1. Thonging chisel to open diamond-shaped stitching holes; 2. Round awl to trace leather; 3. PVC mat to use with the thonging chisel; 4. Felt mat to lay out under the PVC mat; 5. Wooden mallet to hammer the chisel.

1 All the cardinal stitches (start and end point of a seam, the angles, etc.) should be opened with the round awl.

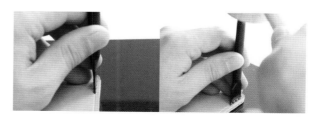

2 Place the chisel vertically on the leather and punch it with the wooden mallet. If your holes are slanting, you won't be able to properly sew your leather.

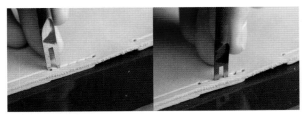

3 If there is little space between two cardinal points, take a two-pronged chisel and try to open holes in an even and balanced way.

4 For straight lines, open your holes with a four-pronged chisel. You just need to insert the first prong in the last hole made and pierce the leather.

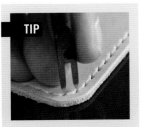

5 If you have about 10 slits left before your next cardinal point, first trace lightly the position of all the remaining 10 slits, adjust them, and then pierce them.

TIP

For curved angles, use a one- or two-pronged chisel to achieve a curved stitching line.

6 We have opened all the holes we need for lacing the leather. Make sure they are all pierced.

STITCHING THE LEATHER

We usually wax a linen thread to sew the leather, but you can instead use already-waxed nylon thread in the color of your choice.

THINGS YOU'LL NEED

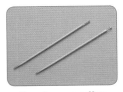

Sewing needles
Many kinds are available, but you will usually find the round and thin ones in the kits.

Thread
The craft sets normally include a medium linen thread, which needs to be waxed.

Wax
To be used with the thread. This makes it stronger and more durable.

1 Although it varies slightly with the thickness of the thread, the amount of lace needed for this stitch is 4 to 5 times the distance to be laced.

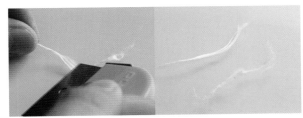

2 Thin the end of the thread with your knife. It will be very easy to thread the needle once the thread is waxed.

3 Press the thread on the wax down firmly and drag across. Turn it over and repeat the process until the thread has become as stiff as the picture above right.

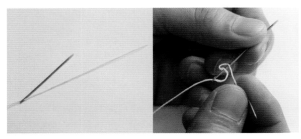

4 Thread your first needle, and then pierce the thread twice as in the above right picture.

5 Pull the thread all the way back. You'll see that it will have formed a knot. Twist it to lock it in place.

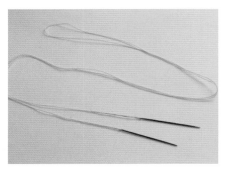

6 Repeat the same steps for the other end of your thread and you are ready to stitch!

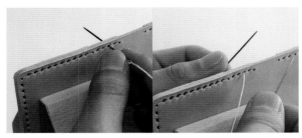

7 Place your piece of leather so that the left side is the reverse. We usually start from the third slit, stitching backward and then stitching regularly. Pull the needle through the third hole until you are at the center of the thread.

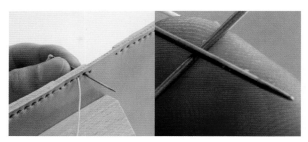

8 Push needle 1 (in your left hand) through slit no.2 while holding needle 2 (in your right hand) behind it.

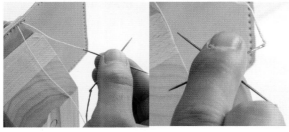

9 Once you pulled it through, hold both needles in your right hand (above left) and twist your hand toward you (above right).

10 Push needle 2 through the same hole as the thread. Don't pierce the thread!

11 Pull the stitch tight. Repeat the same steps until you reach slit no.1. Your ease of sewing will depend a lot on the stiffness and thickness of the leather.

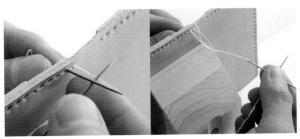

12 Now start stitching toward you. You should follow the same steps, pushing the left needle in slit no.2.

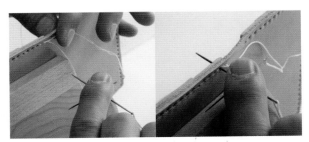

13 You then twist your hand and push the right needle through the same hole.

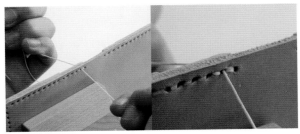

14 Make sure you repeat the previous steps to sew the whole seam.

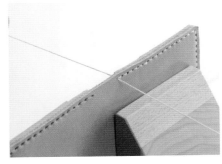

15 When you are finished, backstitch two holes in the direction where you started.

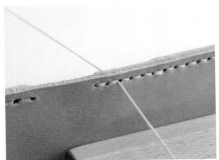

16 This is how you should end your stitches.

17 Cut your threads close to the leather.

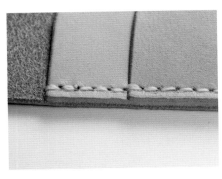

18 This is how properly sewn leather should look.

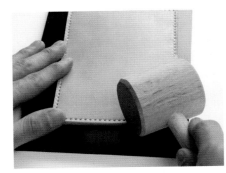

19 Even up the stitches and press them into shape with the side of a mallet.

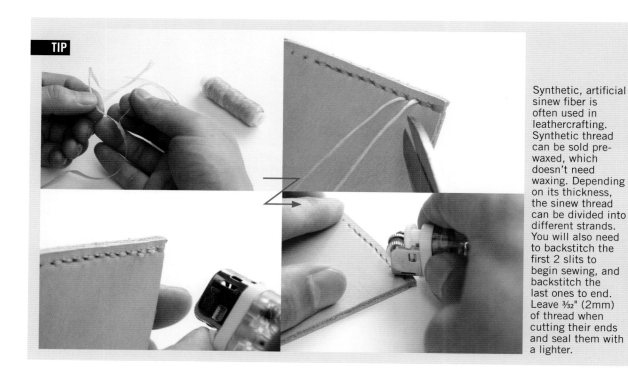

Synthetic, artificial sinew fiber is often used in leathercrafting. Synthetic thread can be sold pre-waxed, which doesn't need waxing. Depending on its thickness, the sinew thread can be divided into different strands. You will also need to backstitch the first 2 slits to begin sewing, and backstitch the last ones to end. Leave ³⁄₃₂" (2mm) of thread when cutting their ends and seal them with a lighter.

HOW TO FINISH THE EDGES

After you finished sewing your item, you will need to burnish its edges. This means you will need to bevel them, file them, apply a finish, and burnish them.

1 Use a beveler to get slick, round edges.

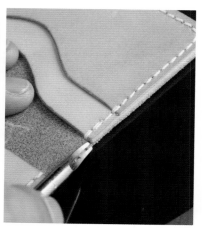

2 Bevel all the edges, including the other side.

3 File the side with a sanding stick to get a flat, even surface.

4 File the beveled edges too to get a rounder look.

5 Apply glossing polish to the edges only. If the finish goes on the grain side, it will stain it and stay there.

TIP

If you want to dye the edges, do it before you apply the finish. Apply the dye as evenly as possible with a cotton swab.

6 Rub the finished edges with a hard surface, like a bone folder. Do both angles and the side.

Beveled edges should look like this. If you'd like to dye them, use a darker color than the leather to get a more professional look.

Done!

How to Lace

Together with hand-stitching, lacing is one of the core skills to know when leather crafting. It can also be used as an ornament. Either way, it will have a great impact on your item. Here are tutorials on the "whipstitch" and the "double-loop stitch." Pay attention as to whether you will start and finish lacing at the same point or at separate points.

THINGS YOU'LL NEED

Thonging chisels
Opens the slits that you will lace. The prongs should be the same size as the lace.

Lacing awl
Multipurpose. Can open slits and enlarge existing holes.

2-prong lacing needle
Match the size of the needle's eye with the width of your lace.

Lace
We use a ³⁄₃₂" to ⅛" (2 to 3mm)-wide cowhide lace. It should fit your needle.

Wooden mallet
Used to open slits or even out your stitches.

LACING: THE BASICS

You should learn how a two-pronged needle is threaded. It is also indispensable for you to know how to stick two pieces of lace together, in case you run out of lace during your work.

▶ **Threading your needle**

1 Pare off a ¹⁹⁄₃₂" (1.5cm) tip, and cut both sides to get a thin, pointed tip.

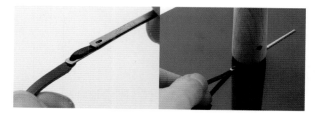

2 Open the needle and insert the tip in the needle, smooth side up, threading the first hole from underneath. Close the needle with a light mallet tap. To remove the lace, just spring open the needle.

▶ **Sticking two laces together**

1 If you run out of lace during your project, pare a ¹³⁄₃₂" (1cm) tip on the grain side of the lace you were using, and ¹³⁄₃₂" (1cm) off the flesh side of the new lace.

2 Apply glue on both pared ends and glue them together. Press firmly together with the mallet.

OPENING THE SLITS

This works the same way as opening stitching holes for hand-sewing. It's as easy as using a wooden hammer to drive the thonging chisel through the leather and open slits.

▶ Opening the cardinal points

1 These points should be opened with a one-pronged chisel and include the slits on the edge where there are different layers. First, mark them with the lacing awl.

2 Then, open the slit with the one-pronged chisel. Take care not to pierce the extra layer on the back. It is easier if you are using a scrap of leather for support.

3 Other cardinal points include the corners. Using a two-pronged chisel as a guide, mark with the lacing awl where the slits should be opened, and open them with a one-pronged chisel.

4 These are the cardinal points that had to be opened on this item.

▶ The other slits

1 Use a three-pronged chisel to open slits on a straight line.

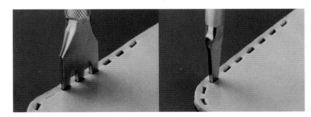

2 Sometimes it's easier to finish the job with a two- or one-pronged chisel.

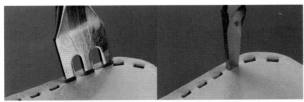

3 As you can see in the above left picture, you might end up not having enough space to make your slits with a three-pronged chisel. In this case, take a one-pronged chisel, lightly mark the remaining slits, and open them if they look balanced with the other slits.

4 By adjusting the spacing between your slits a little, you should end up with something like this. Make sure the slits are not too close to each other, or they might rip later on.

THE WHIPSTITCH

This is a very simple stitch, but it will take some practice to lace a professional-looking stitch. It is essentially a lace that spirals around the edge of your item. There are two ways of doing this, one for projects with a separate beginning and ending, and another for common start and end points. The amount of lace required is three times the distance to be laced.

▶ **Whipstitch no.1 (common start and end points)**

1 Before you start lacing, finish off the edges of your item.

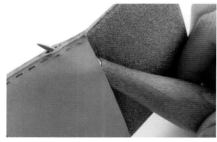

2 To hide the beginning of your lacing, open a small space between the layers of your first slit.

3 Then begin lacing, starting in between the layers of leather, from the space you just opened. Leave about ¹³⁄₃₂" (1cm) at the end.

4 Lace as shown. Make sure the lace doesn't twist, place the end underneath the loop, and pull the lace until you lock it.

5 Push the needle into the second hole and pull your lace tight. Repeat this step until you reach your first stitch.

6 Push your needle in your last stitch as shown, pull the needle from between the layers of leather, and pass it through your last loop. Pull it tight until you lock your lace.

7 Carefully cut your end close to the stitches. Apply glue on both ends, and push the lace in between the layers of leather with the lacing awl to hide them.

8 Last step: Press the stitches into shape with your wooden mallet.

▶ Whipstitch no.2 (separate start and end points)

1 Open a small space between the layers of leather close to your first slit.

2 Push the needle in between those layers and the first slit, pull, and push it into the slit opposite the first one. Then push again into your very first slit. Leave 13/32" (1cm) at the end.

3 Push the needle into the second slit, and before you tighten the lace, cut the end close to the edge and apply glue to fix it.

4 Pull the lace and continue lacing, tightening as you go.

▶ Ending

1 Before you lace your last slits, open a space between the layers of leather.

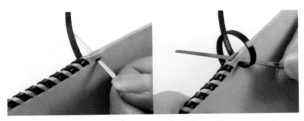

2 Push the needle through your last two slits as usual, but before tightening, push the needle one more time through the first slit and then between the layers and through the loop.

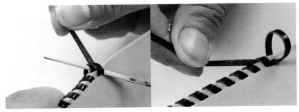

3 You can now tighten the loop and pull the needle to lock your stitch.

4 Cut the lace close to the edge, apply glue, and hide the lace with the lacing awl.

DOUBLE-LOOP STITCH

Although more complicated than the whipstitch, you just need to learn how to lace one stitch and then you are done. One important thing to keep in mind is to always use the same strength when tightening the lace. This stitch uses seven to eight times more lace than the length of the project.

▶ **Double-loop stitch no.1 (common start and end points)**

1 Start stitching where the ends of the stitch can be discreetly hidden. Begin on the front side, and after pulling out the needle, hook the lace around the end like shown.

2 Lock the hooked lace by pushing the needle through your second slit on the front side and tightening it.

3 Bring the lace in the front and push the needle under the crossed section. Tighten the lace.

4 Just repeat the previous steps: lace through the next stitch, push under the cross, and pull the lace snug. Make sure you always have the grain side of the lace facing outward.

5 Before lacing your last slits, pull the beginning of the lace out of the loop (left) from the front side, and pull it again out of the front slit and up between the layers of leather (right). You should have one slit left on the back and two on the front.

6 Cut close the end of the lace that you just pulled out, tuck it between the layers, and glue it there. Now, lace the next slit, bring the lace to the front, and lace the loop. You should have only one slit left to lace.

7 From the front, push the needle through the last cross-section, and then from the back side, push your needle just like in the above left picture.

8 From the front side, push the needle through the last slit and in between the layers and out between the lacing as shown. Cut off the end of the lace and tuck it inside the lacing.

▶ **Double-loop stitch no.2 (separate start and end points)**

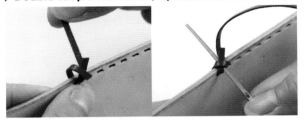 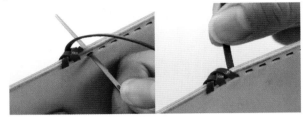

1 Lace the first slit from the front side and pull from the back slit. Tighten your lace over the tip of the lace. This will form a cross. Push the needle to the back under the cross and tighten the lace.

2 You just need to repeat the previous step until your last slit. Lace the next slit, pull it tight, and push the needle under the last cross and pull tight.

▶ **Ending**

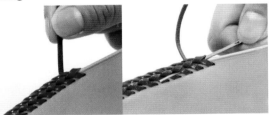 

1 Lace your last stitch as usual, pulling the needle from under the last crossed section, then push the needle in between the lacing, as shown.

2 Once you've pulled your lace out, cut the lace close to the stitches and tuck it inside. That's it!

▶ **Lacing corners**

1 When lacing a corner, you should lace the same hole a few times to prevent spacing between the lacing. Open the corner slit with a size 1 (2.1mm) drive punch tool to allow space for those multiple stitches.

2 The first time, lace the corner slit as usual (left). After you've pulled the needle from under the cross, lace again the corner slit (right) and then push the lace under the last crossed section.

3 You will lace the corner stitch a third time (left), and after going through the cross, lace the next slit as normal (right).

4 Depending on the type of curve, you might want to stitch the corner slit either once or twice. This will prevent gaps in the lacing.

Machine-Sewing

A sewing machine not only speeds up your work, it also widens the type of projects you will be able to create. As you can also sew the linings for your items, with a sewing machine you will be able to sew to your heart's content. But because leather tends to be thicker and more resistant than cloth, make sure that your machine has enough power to handle leather.

THINGS YOU'LL NEED

Rubber cement
We need to use a weaker type of glue to prevent the needles from damaging.

Sewing machine needles for leather
These are chisel-pointed needles. Match the size of the needle to your thread.

Upholstery-weight thread
Choose a heavy-duty, pure nylon or polyester thread.

SEWING MACHINE SETTINGS

You will use your sewing machine in the same way as you use it to sew cloth. The points below are just things worth remembering when sewing.

▶ Stitch length

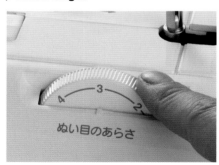

Adjust your settings so that your stitch length is 2.5–3mm when sewing leather.

▶ Stitch patterns

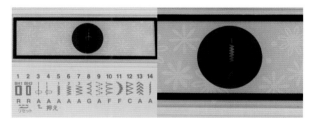

When stitching a straight seam, you can use whichever pattern is easiest for you. Use the zigzag seam when stitching an appliqué, and choose the size you think would look best.

▶ Sewing different layers together

Make sure that the stitches are not too close to the border and won't rip the leather. Stitch over the most vulnerable area at least three times.

▶ Flattening the seams

Seams tend to overlay thick materials like leather. To flatten them, just gently stroke the seams with your wooden mallet.

BACKSTITCHING

When sewing leather, you will usually backstitch both at the start and at the end of your seam. It will strengthen the seam, so it is important that you don't skip this step.

1 Put the needle down into your fabric where you want to begin.

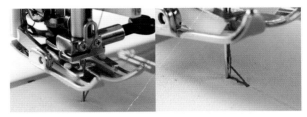

2 Sew two stitches forward, and then push the backstitch button (or lever or knob), hold it down, and start sewing again to your starting point. You can now sew as usual.

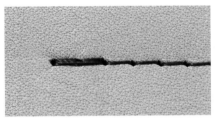 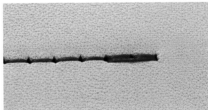

3 Follow the same steps to backstitch your last stitches, but backward. To lock your seam, follow the instructions below.

SEALING THE SEAM

It's easier to seal the threads with a machine-sewn seam than a hand-sewn one. There are two ways: one where the threads end up on the flesh side, and the other where they are on the grain side.

▶ **Locking your seam on the flesh side**

1 You can simply pull your threads to have them on the same side (flesh side).

2 Cut your threads, leaving a short tip, and apply flex glue to lock the seams to your leather.

▶ **Using a lighter to seal the seam**

1 When both threads are on the grain side, cut their ends to a 3/16" (5mm) tip.

2 Gently use the lighter to melt your synthetic thread, and press it into shape while it is still warm.

Fasteners: The Basics

Here, we will explain how to set the most commonly used fasteners in leather crafting. These include heavy-duty snaps, segma snaps, and ball closures. To rivet these, you will need riveting tools, which can be different depending on the type and size of fastener you are using. It's also good to learn about the differences between the fasteners so that you'll be able to choose the best one for your project.

THINGS YOU'LL NEED

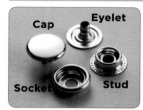

Generally, two sizes are available: large and medium. The eyelet and stud will go on the main part of the item, while the cap and socket go on the cover. The snaps are not made for thin leather, because you need a lot of force to set the snap.

The setter has to be one that goes with this type of snap and size.

HOW TO SET A HEAVY-DUTY SNAP

These snaps are commonly used for fastening wallets and bags. They need a few good whacks to be set in place.

▶ **Eyelet and stud**

1 Chose a drive punch tool the size of the post of the eyelet and open the hole where you will set the male parts in.

2 Push the post in the hole, making sure it's on the right side.

3 The post should stick ³⁄₃₂"–⅛" (2–3mm) out of the leather. After placing the eyelet on top, it should be just poking out slightly.

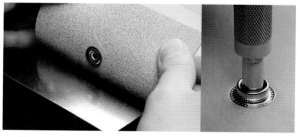

4 Place the leather on a hard surface and tap the snap with the setter and mallet.

5 The post should flatten, holding the eyelet in place.

▶ **Cap and socket**

6 With the same drive punch tool, open the hole where you will place the other side of the snap. The cap's post should stick out of the socket.

7 Place the snap on the anvil and tap the setter with the mallet.

8 Check that the two snaps fasten and don't rattle.

HOW TO SET A SEGMA SNAP

This is perhaps the most common type of fastener you can find in leather crafting. It is very easy to use, but because of its shortness it can only be set on leather thinner than 3/32" (2mm).

WHAT YOU'LL NEED

Cap   Eyelet
Socket   Stud

Stud setter
Socket setter

These snaps are available in various sizes and need to be whacked by two different setters that can also vary in size.

1 Open the hole where you'll place your eyelet. The hole should be the size of the post.

2 Place the eyelet underneath and cover it with the stud.

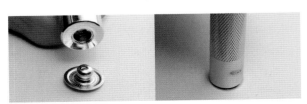

3 Place the glove or stud snap setter and tap it a few times.

4 You know you've done a good job when the snaps fit tightly together.

5 Open the hole where you will set your socket. The hole size should match the post's size.

6 Set the two pieces on the leather, and position the cap on the anvil.

7 Use a setter for the socket and do the same—tap the socket until it is in place. Make sure the socket is set against the leather when you are doing this.

8 Make sure they don't shake.

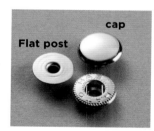

9 Check that they snap together fine.

cap

Flat post

10 Depending on the item you are crafting, you can also replace the cap with a flat post.

HOW TO SET A BALL SCREW CLOSURE

This is also a popular fastener for leather items, especially with vegetable-tanned leather. It is often used to close flaps, but because it is a discreet fastener it is also screwed on carved items.

THINGS YOU'LL NEED

A screw-on ball stud.

A small leather knife and a flat-head screwdriver.

▶ **Screwing the ball stud**

1 The hole you will open to set the socket in should be the same size as the screw.

2 Insert the screw from the reverse side of the leather. Sometimes you need to force it in.

3 The screw should be poking out of the leather.

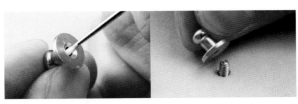

4 Apply flex glue in the cavity of the ball stud and screw it on the socket.

5 Finish screwing with the screwdriver.

6 The stud should look like this. If it is "sinking" into the leather, you have screwed it too much.

▶ **Opening the receiving end**

> The size of the receiving end will depend on the leather's thickness and the size of the ball stud. Here, the stud is ¼" (6mm) big and the leather ³⁄₃₂"–⅛" (2–3mm) thick.

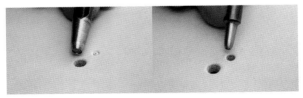

7 When your stud is ¼" (6mm) big, create two dots that are ⁵⁄₁₆" (7.5mm) apart, as shown

8 We will use a ⁵⁄₃₂" dia and a ⁵⁄₆₄" dia drive punch tool to open these receiving holes.

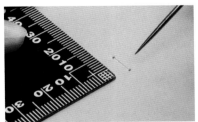

9 Open the holes.

10 Link the holes with a cut, as shown.

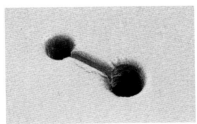

11 This is how the ball stud's receiving end should look.

12 Close and open the fasteners a few times. It will be a little tough to close it at the beginning, but you will see that with a little time the leather will loosen up.

Message for Leather Crafters

Crafters' Comments

Go with your guts and create the things you want!

The business card holder on page 116 was designed to highlight the seams and the clean-cut shape of the leather. The point here is to choose a wider-spaced thonging chisel and combine it with a thicker thread. Work with vegetable-tanned leather so that with time your card holder will age and have a golden glow. Keep its look minimal, with simple ornaments—here you can use a silver concha—or personalize it further with any of the ornamental techniques presented in the Decorative Techniques section. We recommend branding your initials with leather pyrography. You can get inspired from American motorcycle and rock subcultures or tattoo designs.

Use a thinner type of leather for the tote bag to avoid having to make it softer. Your options will also increase if you can learn how to create inner pockets and a lining.

For people who have just started with leather crafting, try not to strive for perfection but instead make sure you try different techniques to widen the breadth of your skills.

Ikkei Kobayashi
An old hand at the art of leathercraft, he specializes in rock and biker culture. In this book, he is in charge of a wide variety of projects that range from delicate to free-form shapes.

Being surprised and getting excited with leather crafting

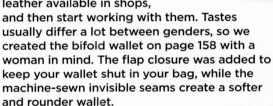

Chrome leather is often used for more feminine items, but these can also be created with vegetable-tanned leather. First, get used to the differences in the leather available in shops, and then start working with them. Tastes usually differ a lot between genders, so we created the bifold wallet on page 158 with a woman in mind. The flap closure was added to keep your wallet shut in your bag, while the machine-sewn invisible seams create a softer and rounder wallet.

One of the pleasures of making something by hand is to be able to carefully choose the materials and techniques to be used. I want you to take your time and enjoy that process.

One advice on colors: Choosing the same color for your hide and thread is perfectly fine, but if you are undecided, try to get a thread that is one tone lighter than the hide. Also, a beige thread will go with almost any color hide.

Sometimes you won't like how a project looks. I would suggest trying it out, as you might end up liking it—and at the same time discover new designs and techniques!

Megumi Hoshi
Very skillful with a sewing machine, she often creates cute and pretty objects with it. In this book, she is in charge of the most feminine items and the babouches.

Decorative Techniques

Here, the foundations for typical ornament techniques are introduced.

Dyeing

This tutorial teaches you how to pigment leather with craft dye. All you need to start is a paintbrush and dye. Natural leather can be dyed in a wide range of colors. Here, we will show you how to dye different shades with only one color.

THINGS YOU'LL NEED
- Craft dye
- Good-quality masking tape
- Paintbrush

1 Work on top of an old newspaper. Lightly wet the surface of your piece of leather. The water should only leave a faint trace.

2 Cut masking tape in the size that you want, stick it on the leather, and squeeze out the bubbles and creases.

3 After you've arranged the masking tape, soak the leather once more. In a small bowl, dilute 5 times your craft dye for your first layer.

4 Dye the leather in swift, sweeping movements to get a uniform result. Change direction and apply a few more layers.

5 Pat dry the excess dye on the masking tape, change the stained newspaper to a new one, and let the leather dry naturally. If you use a dryer, it can cause the masking tape to become more sticky, thus making it harder to remove.

6 After you've dried it, apply the second layer of masking tape.

7 Add more dye in the preparation to create a darker shade.

8 Follow steps 4 and 5.

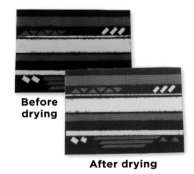

9 If the flesh side can be seen on your item, dye it too.

Before drying

After drying

10 The color will become lighter once the leather has dried. You can also apply a coating to avoid tarnishing the leather. Dye the leather before you use it for your projects, because it can shrink a little during the process.

▶ **Dyeing leather laces**

It's easy to dye a leather lace. Just pour some dye in a small container, slowly dip the lace in the dye, and then remove any excess dye with water. Let it then dry on a piece of newspaper. This method will allow you to get more colored laces than there are on the market.

Leather Pyrography

Much easier than it sounds, leather pyrography is simply a drawing or motif etched with a heated metal implement. Classic tattoo designs are very popular for this type of craft, from which you can draw inspiration and create your own designs. Tracing on the leather can be a little tricky, so practice beforehand and then have fun! For this tutorial, we have burned the Business Card Holder from page 116.

Crafter: Tomoaki Motoyama

THINGS YOU'LL NEED
- Solid-point burner with heat adjustment
- Stylus
- Tracing paper

1 Once you have drawn your design in the correct size, copy it onto tracing paper with a pencil. Mark the shadows with dotted lines.

2 Before tracing the design onto the leather, lightly wet it to soften it.

3 Hold the tracing paper in place with a paperweight, and trace the contours onto the leather with a stylus. Press lightly.

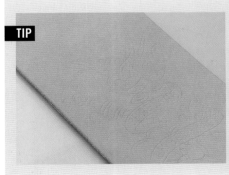

TIP

The traces should be faint but visible to the eye. Pyrography might be more difficult if the trace lines are too strong. Dot the shadows, too.

4 We will use our finest point in order to trace a delicate pattern. Set the temperature to medium (6 or 7) and do a test on a scrap of leather.

5 Instead of burning the drawing by portions, draw the outline first and then go into more detail.

6 Sparsely dot the leather to create shadows. Just lightly touch the leather, otherwise you will end up with a bold dot.

7 As errors are not removable, start by sparsely dotting the whole design, and with an eye on the balance of the picture, add dots as needed.

8 When adding more dots, you can press your burner a little longer to get a darker burn.

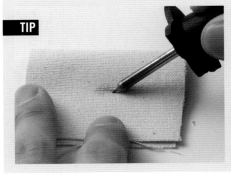

TIP

Regularly clean the tip on a heat-resistant cloth.

These are generally the three steps to go through in this type of work. You will first draw an outline of your drawing, then start dotting it to create light shadows, and finally add the darker shades to give it life. Pyrography does not allow for errors, so make sure to practice on scraps first.

Stitches, Appliqués, and Punching

This tutorial will teach you how to sew appliqués on leather, to create ornamental stitches with your sewing machine, and to use the shape-punch tool. Since these techniques are easy to learn, this project is especially suitable for beginners. We used the Bifold Wallet from page 158.

Crafter: Megumi Hoshi

THINGS YOU'LL NEED
- Sewing machine
- Tracing paper
- Shape leather punch set

▶ **Stitching**

1 Cut the tracing paper in the shape of your leather and draw a simple stitching design in the position you want it to be. Ours was inspired by trees.

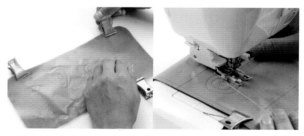

2 Clip it on the piece of leather and machine-sew over the design in the color of your choice.

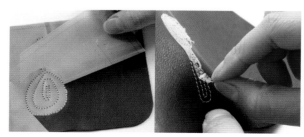

3 When you are finished sewing all the lines, rip out the tracing paper bit by bit. If you force it, you risk tearing the thread with the paper.

TIP

For a great result, try to use colors in the same tonality or that complement each other. We used three colors.

▶ **Appliqués**

1 We will create appliqués in the shape of a sheep. The leather disc is the body, while the rounded cross is the head.

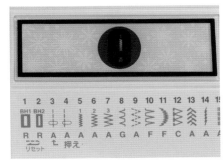

2 We will use the zigzag stitch to sew the appliqués. Set the size to one that is suitable for your pieces of leather.

3 First stitch the head onto the body. It will be easier to machine-sew small pieces by laying a piece of paper underneath that will be ripped out after you've sewn the head.

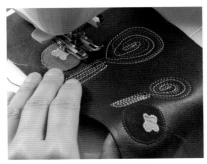

4 Then stitch the sheep on your piece of leather. It is not necessary to glue it, but it could be a good idea to affix it temporarily on the leather before starting sewing.

▶ **Punching**

1 You will just need shape-punch tools to open holes in the leather. These come in various shapes, such as stars, hearts, and diamonds.

2 When gluing the piece of leather behind the holes, don't glue the holes too!

3 Flatten the leather with a wooden mallet.

By freely arranging different patterns together, you should be able to create many personalized items!

Done!

Leather Carving

It is often said that carving is one of the finest techniques in leathercraft. This is the art of stamping and carving the surface to give it a three-dimensional appearance. But carving an item is not a project you can complete in one day, and you will definitely need a lot of practice before feeling confident with this craft. For those of you interested in carving, we suggest you read more literature on it.

Crafter: Seiichi Koyashiki

We have carved this pattern on the Medium-Sized Wallet from page 144. As you can see for yourself, the wallet gives a completely different impression once it has been carved.

THINGS YOU'LL NEED

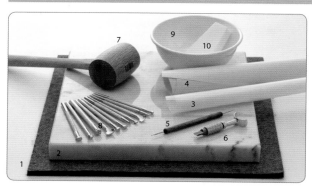

We will also use (left to right): leather finish; antique dye; leather dye.

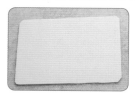

Before working the leather, you need to case it by moistening it with a sponge. Then stick masking tape on the back to prevent the leather from deforming and avoid letting the leather dry out.

1. Felt mat; 2. Block of marble; 3. Tracing paper; 4. Good-quality masking tape; 5. Double-point stylus; 6. Swivel knife; 7. Wooden mallet; 8. Stamps; 9. Bowl; 10. Sponge.
We will also use water and a mechanical pencil. The types of stamps will depend on the pattern used.

LEATHER CARVING TUTORIAL

Although this is a very short introduction to carving, it will show you the steps that need to be undertaken to carve leather.

▶ **Leather preparation**

1 Trace the pattern onto the tracing paper. Double-check that you haven't forgotten anything.

2 Position the tracing paper on the cased leather and trace the pattern with the stylus.

3 Compare your transfer with the original pattern and see if you have everything copied.

▶ **Carving the pattern**

1 First cut the border with the swivel knife.

2 The round cut should be done in two turns.

3 The petals should be carved by turning the blade.

4 Gradually reduce the depth of the cut for any lines that do not join another line.

▶ **Beveler tool**

You bevel by striking the tool along the cut lines. To avoid leaving tool marks, bevel with smooth movements, as if you were gliding on the leather. By "raising" the leather, it will help highlight the flowers and the leaves.

▶ **Camouflage tool**

This will give a three-dimensional appearance to the stalks of the leather. You can achieve a variety of patterns depending on the angle of the tool.

▶ Shader tool

The shader is used to add shade to petals, leaves, and their contours.

▶ Veiner tool

This is a stamp used to pattern leaves and flowers. When creating the veins of the plant, use the veiner on one side and the camouflage on the other for a better result.

▶ Seeder tool

This is primarily used to create the flower centers and embellish the scroll ends. Use it lightly.

▶ Mulesfoot tool

This is used to add texture to the flowers' stems. Change the angle of the tool to get a different impression.

▶ Backgrounder tool

This is used to dim or mat the background areas, thus highlighting the foreground.

▶ Matting tool

This is commonly used to mat down the areas that are outside the pattern, like between two patterns.

▶ Decorative cuts

Using the swivel knife, decorative cuts are used to show the character of your designs. The cuts should be light and should end smoothly.

▶ Dye the background

With a brush, dye the portions you matted with the backgrounder tool. This will help draw attention to the other parts of your carving.

▶ Color and finish

1 Apply a coat of leather finish to the surface with a piece of cloth. This will prevent applying too much antique dye.

2 Rub the antique dye with an old toothbrush.

3 Wipe the dye with the dried cloth and reapply the finish.

Done!

The antique dye will remain on the stamped leather and help bring out the shadows and highlight the details of your carving. Reapplying another coat of leather finish will help fix the antique dye.

Message for Leather Crafters

Crafters' Comments

Relax and enjoy!

One of the things I enjoy most with this craft is the ability we develop to work with a raw material like leather. You learn how to fiddle with it and then mold it in your desired shape. Leather has a malleability that few other materials possess, and its organic texture is just a pleasure to work with for your senses.

Then, of course, leather also allows you to create items that you can use and enjoy every day for years to come. Leather's unique properties also mean that, if treated with care, it will age very well.

Once you develop a basic know-how of this art, you will also start taking pleasure in choosing the various materials needed for your project. As you'll see, something as minor as the color of the thread can dramatically change the appearance of your item. When hand-sewing, you will also have to carefully balance the thickness of the thread with the width of the thonging chisel. The quality and type of leather will also have an impact on your finished product. All of this also means that, when choosing your material and while creating your item, you must keep in mind the end result you are striving for.

As designers and creators of this book, we all want you to feel the pleasure we took in creating these projects. So please relax and enjoy what you are doing!

Have a clear objective and work toward it patiently.

Learning leather crafting requires patience and a lot of perseverance. This is an art for which you will need a lot of practice in order to master it.

Sometimes things won't go as you expected them to—but instead of stressing about it and losing your temper, try spending a little more time on it, or put it aside and work on it the next day, and eventually you will be able to resolve the issue.

Just like any other craft, in order to really understand and make the most out of leather craft, you will need to invest yourself in it. You will need to make sure that you have the right tools and enough time to finish the project. You will need to keep stress low and take things slowly. You will need to try out as many things and techniques as possible—regardless of whether you like the project or not. You might not be able to make what you want immediately. First learn the techniques, and then—and only then— improvise and have fun. These are the best pieces of advice I have to offer.

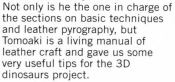

Tomoaki Motoyama
Not only is he the one in charge of the sections on basic techniques and leather pyrography, but Tomoaki is a living manual of leather craft and gave us some very useful tips for the 3D dinosaurs project.

Seiichi Koyashiki
A senior teacher in leathercrafting, Sensei Koyashiki is the mind and the hand behind the delicate yet dynamic design of the leather carving presented on the preceding pages.

No-Sew Items

In order to study the characteristic of leather, and the fundamental way of treating, it starts with making an easy leather item.

Tools Used in Step 1

In this part of the book, we will craft leather without sewing it. This section has been created for those who would like to make something with leather without stitching it. Some projects will only require cutting the leather and polishing it, while others will also need some glue. Vegetable tanned leather can, thanks to its elasticity, also be used to make beautiful shapes. This is done by soaking it in water, molding it, and drying it. If you try each of these projects, you will quickly improve your leather-crafting skills.

THINGS YOU'LL NEED TO CUT LEATHER

The first thing you will need to do is cut the pieces out. You can either do it with a leather knife or, if the leather is thin enough, scissors. For those who are not yet used to the leather knife, you can use a steel square to cut out straight lines.

Round mawl
To transfer the reference points of the paper pattern to the leather, or to mark the placement of holes before opening them.

Scissors
Although they cannot be used with thick leather, you will be able to finely cut thinner hides.

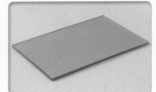

PVC cutting mat
To be used when cutting leather. Its thickness and elasticity will prevent the blade from damaging the work surface.

Leather knife (Japanese style shown here)
The blade can be exchanged easily once it becomes blunt. In this book we use the leather knife as a basic tool.

Framing square
L-shaped and made out of aluminium or steel, it can be used as a ruler or as a guide for knives and cutters.

THINGS YOU'LL NEED TO PUNCH HOLES

The round drive punch tool will not be included in a starter's kit because the size of your holes will vary according to your project. You will have to buy them as you need them.

Rubber mat
Working over a rubber mat will allow the tools to cut deep enough to make a clean-cut hole without dulling the tools.

Felt mat
If laid under the rubber mat, it will help dampen the noises of the mallet and the drive punch tool.

Wooden mallet
A wooden mallet strikes the drive punch tool and other metallic tools, like the thonging chisel (Step 2), without damaging them. Can also be used for crimping (pressing together).

Round drive punch tool
Place the tool where you would like to open the hole, and punch the leather with the strike of a wooden mallet.

THINGS YOU'LL NEED TO GLUE

In Step 1, items are glued together instead of being stitched. In the basic tool kit, you will most often find a water-based adhesive that needs to be used before it dries. But depending on the project, sometimes you will need adhesive that needs to be half-dried before the leather is glued together.

Glue applicator stick
To apply glue smoothly and thinly on leather. The starter's kits usually provide a ²⁵⁄₃₂" (20mm)-wide stick, but for larger surfaces you can also purchase a 1 ¹¹⁄₄" (40mm)-wide applicator.

Flex glue
Water-based adhesive that is white when applied and dries clear and flexible. Non-toxic, with very little smell. Apply to both sides and bond before it dries.

Super glue
Fast-setting, strong bond adhesive. Surfaces need to be bonded before glue dries. The glue contains solvent, so ventilate your workshop when using it.

Roller
When rolled over glued leather pieces, it helps seal them together. It will crimp the leather without damaging it.

THINGS YOU'LL NEED TO BURNISH EDGES

Smoothing and polishing the edges of the leather can make the leather look better and be more wear-resistant. Finishing off the edges is an important step in making a high-quality item. Although we suggest using a plastic bone folder, you can try other methods and see which one suits your taste.

Sanding stick
With thin and coarser grit paper on each side, it is used to sand and polish the edges after they have been beveled.

Edge beveler
This bevels and rounds off edges after the leather has been glued. To achieve a smooth outcome, sand the beveled edges.

Plastic bone folder
An efficient and basic tool used to rub and smooth the edges. Can also be used to create creases and folded lines.

Glossing polish
A polishing agent to be used before the plastic bone folder is rubbed on the edges and flesh side. It will flatten fuzzy leather.

Tassels

Tassels can be used anywhere, for flair on bags and purses, on zipper pulls, and of course as key rings. These can easily be made with scraps of leather, so they are a perfect project for beginners. With three different layers of leather, they also look a little more special than the ones you ordinarily see.

Hint

It is fun and easy to change the color and feel of the three overlapping pieces of leather that make these tassels. When changing the thickness of the leather, pay attention to the change in balance of the tassel. We recommend you use the more pliable chrome leather, but vegetable-tanned leather will be fine too.

WHAT YOU'LL NEED
- Because we want to keep the softness of the leather, we will use the flex glue.

LEATHER USED
- A: Chrome-tanning leather (camel)
- B: Chrome-tanning leather (beige)
- C: Chrome-tanning leather (bright beige)

Crafter: Megumi Hoshi
▶ Paper pattern: page 171

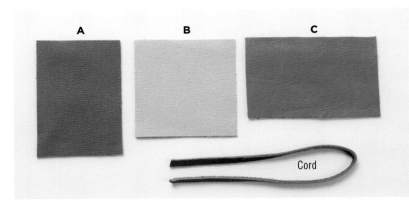

1 A–C will be used for the body of the tassel. Each piece has a different length and width, so please check their shape against the paper pattern. The ⁵⁄₃₂" x 10" (4 x 250mm) cord can be cut out from a scrap of leather.

2 Take the grain side where the glue will be applied and abrade a ⅜" (5mm) strip on pieces A and B to give some grip to the glue (piece C will be done later).

3 Cut ³⁄₃₂" (2mm)-wide strips on all pieces of leather, leaving uncut the strip for the glue. The fringe can be cut approximately, but if you want more precision please refer to the paper pattern.

4 Align the folded cord with A. Mark where glue will be applied on the cord at the same height of A's uncut strip. In the picture, it will be 2 ½" to 2 ¾" (65 to 70mm) from the end of the cord.

5 Glue together the marks on the flesh sides of the cord with some flex glue. Be careful not to twist the cord.

6 Abrade the marks on the grain side of the cord and apply some flex glue.

7 Apply flex glue on both sides of A's uncut strip and wait until it is no longer sticky.

8 Affix the cord on one end of the flesh side of A and begin rolling the fringed piece around the cord. Use a round awl to help you.

9 Apply glue on both sides of piece B and, starting from one end, roll it around piece A.

10 Before applying flex glue to piece C, roll it once around the tassel and mark where the strip will end on C. The part that will show will not be abraded.

11 On the grain side, abrade the glue strip up to the mark you have made in step 10 and apply flex glue. Glue the entire strip on the flesh side and start rolling it around the tassel.

12 Finally, apply some pressure with something hard, like the handle of the wooden mallet.

Done!

You can either use it like this or, if you want, shorten the cord and add a jump ring or other jewelry components.

Leather variations

There are many color variations to chrome- and vegetable-tanned cowhides. When you craft something, you can mix and match the color of the leather with that of the thread and get a customized item. Today, most leather comes from cowhide, but there are less common leathers. If you keep those in mind, you could easily come up with unique leather accessories.

Chrome-tanned leather

Chrome-tanned leather is available in a wide range of colors. The feel, shine, and suppleness are all different from one piece to the next.

Glazed pigskin/pigskin suede

As it stays supple and durable even when it's thinned, pigskin is often used as a lining. One of the most common types of pigskin is the glazed version, where vegetable-tanned leather is polished until the shine comes out. Pigskin suede gets its soft nap from split leather (where the grain has been completely removed).

Corrected grain leather

This is leather where imperfections have been removed and an artificial grain has been embossed into the surface and pigmented with stain or dye. You can emboss almost anything, from woven-bamboo patterns (left) to crocodile imitation leather (right), or dye it to create an "antique" feel or an acrylic one. The shape is preserved by a combination of methods.

Rabbit skins

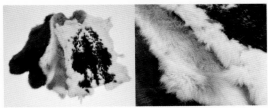

Rabbit skins have a dense, long, and fluffy fur. As it can easily rip, another more resistant hide is used as a lining. As the fur must not be damaged, a lot of care has to go when cutting the skin, which will be cut from the flesh side. Deer, fawn, calf, and mink skins are also available. These furs can give the right accent to the right item.

Deerskin and elk skin

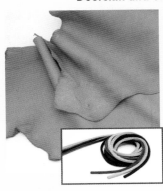

Deerskin leather is soft to the touch, pliable, and able to resist tearing. Because of its unique properties, it is often used for leather laces and cords. Elk skin will have the same characteristics but will be thicker. These skins will perfectly fit your shape and are comfortable to wear.

Exotic leather

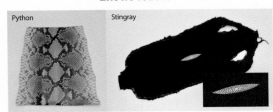

Python   Stingray

Lizard

This category includes the leathers of crocodiles, snakes, rays, ostriches, and lizards. They are difficult to clean and condition and have a very particular grain. They will often be used by luxury brands and are expensive and difficult to buy.

Bracelet
made by cutting and polishing leather

With only these two basic crafting techniques you'll be able to create a leather bracelet. By using vegetable-tanned leather, you'll also enjoy the aging of leather. And you can also decide to use a freehand groover to decorate your bracelet.

Hint

The unique characteristics of leather are enhanced by the simple design of this accessory. We have chosen a ⁵⁄₃₂" (4mm)-thick hide that will add a "biker" feel to your outfit. But remember that the look of this bracelet will change according to the type and thickness of the leather.

Crafter: Tomoaki Motoyama
▶ Paper pattern: page 173

WHAT YOU'LL NEED
- Freehand groover - This tool can cut a groove anywhere on your leather. The depth of the groove will vary with the angle of the blade, so make sure to practice on scraps of leather beforehand.
- Ball closure - (¼" / 6mm). Just screw it on a pre-opened hole.

LEATHER USED
- Cowhide ¼" (4mm) thick
- Oiled cowhide ³⁄₃₂" (2.5mm) thick

ADDITIONAL REQUIREMENT:
- pin or stylus; tracing fpaper

Bracelet

You are finished with merely cutting the leather according to the paper pattern and polishing it. But because the bracelet remains very simple, any errors in crafting it will be visible. So slow down and carefully follow each step.

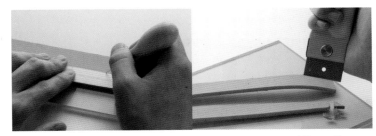

1 Place the paper pattern on the leather and trace around the pattern with a round awl. Using the leather knife, cut roughly around the transferred pattern, leaving a margin.

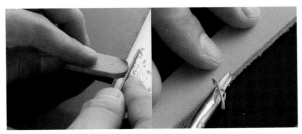

2 File the tips of the bracelet and, with an edge beveler, round off all the edges on both grain and flesh sides.

3 We will now finish off where the red mark is. This step will determine the overall look of the bracelet.

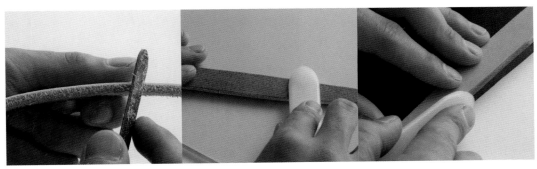

4 With a sanding stick, file the edges and apply glossing polish on both flesh side and cut edges, then rub with a plastic bone folder.

5 The edges should become as smooth as seen in this picture.

6 With the paper pattern, mark the positions of the ball stud and the closure holes.

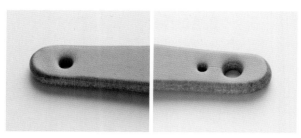

7 Open the stud hole with a ⅛" dia (3.0mm) round drive punch tool, and the closure holes with a ¹⁄₁₆" dia (1.8mm) and ³⁄₁₆" dia (4.5mm).

8 Cut between the two holes to link them.

9 Unscrew the stud, apply some flex glue, and screw the ball stud in the hole.

Done!

With ⁵⁄₃₂" (4mm) thickness, this bracelet is finished after only some polishing.

1 Prepare the design. You can also trace your own pattern.

Engraved Bracelet

Once you have crafted your bracelet, why not use a freehand groover to decorate it? The groover needs to be held in your hand just like a pen, and once you get used to using it, you will be able to carve more refined ornaments on the grain side of your bracelet.

2 With a pencil, transfer the design onto tracing paper. Try to be as precise as possible.

3 Double-check that you have not forgotten to copy any details.

4 Cut the leather according to the paper pattern.

5 Position the tracing paper on the grain side of the leather bracelet and secure it with tape on the flesh side.

6 With a pin or stylus, trace the tracing paper pattern onto the leather.

7 This is how the leather should look. Make sure you haven't forgotten to copy any of the pattern.

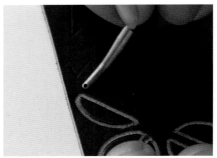

8 With the freehand groover, groove the copied pattern into the leather. Remember that the depth of the groove will change depending on the angle of the blade.

9 Start from an angle and finish in one smooth stroke. Hold it steady and keep the same depth to the groove throughout the pattern.

10 Concentrate on the task at hand, for you won't be able to correct any mistakes.

11 This is how the leather looks when you have finished carving your bracelet.

TIP

Although the design is the same on both bracelets, the different color of the leather will completely change the impression it gives.

12 Polish the edges with a sanding stick and round them off with a beveler.

13 Apply some glossing polish on the flesh side and rub with a plastic bone folder.

14 Burnish the edges using the glossing polish and bone folder.

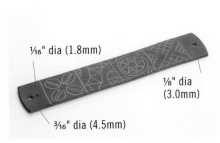

1⁄16" dia (1.8mm)

1⁄8" dia (3.0mm)

3⁄16" dia (4.5mm)

15 Open the three holes required for the closure of the bracelet with a drive punch tool. Cut between the two holes on the left side of the bracelet in the picture.

Done!

16 Unscrew the stud, apply some flex glue, and screw the ball stud into the hole.

Of course, you can design your own pattern on the bracelet!

Charms
made with soft leather

You can easily pin them in your hair or on your blazer, or use it to decorate another item. Made with a soft chrome-tanned leather, you will be able to create a round-looking charm. Because they are so easy to create, you can use scraps of leather to make them anytime.

Hint

We will use a very pliable type of chrome leather, which can stretch a fair bit and has volume too. The flower charm will be created by shrinking the leather with heat. Be careful not to burn yourself!

Crafter: Mayumi Hoshi
▶ Paper pattern: pages 166/172

WHAT YOU'LL NEED

- Alcohol lamp—We will shrink the leather with a small flame. Doing it with a small lighter is complicated, so we will do it with an alcohol lamp that can be used hands-free.
- Brooch pin/clip combo—To be used if you want to pin your charm on your clothes or elsewhere.
- Flex glue
- Contact cement

LEATHER USED

- Pompon charm: Pig suede (blue)
- Flower charm: Chrome-tanning leather (camel)

Pom-Pom Charm

Six leather discs were softly folded and tied up together to create a pom-pom. The basic model will be a semi-sphere, but we will also show you the spherical version. Note that you will have to adjust the quantity of the discs used depending on the thickness of the leather.

Cord

1 The size of the disc will be the size of the pom-pom. You can either follow the paper patterns or choose your own size. Cut out a long cord; we will trim it later.

2 If you are used to handling a leather knife, you can directly cut from the paper pattern. Otherwise, trace the circle on the leather with a pencil and cut it with scissors.

3 Cut out a concentric circle of ⅜" (1cm) in diameter on the paper pattern. Trace it on the leather with a pin or stylus and apply flex glue in the small circle.

4 Lightly fold the disc in four and clip the tip until the glue is dry. Make sure that the outer edges stay slightly open.

5 Open a hole near the tip with a ⁵⁄₃₂" (3.6mm) drive punch tool. Be careful not to open the hole too close to the tip or it will tear.

6 Tie the six folded discs together. When doing so, alternate the direction of the folds to get a more voluminous charm.

7 Using the round awl, pass the leather cord through the holes and bundle the pieces together.

8 Knot the cord twice and apply some flex glue to it.

9 Cut the cord in front of the knot. Adjust the charm's form as desired to complete it.

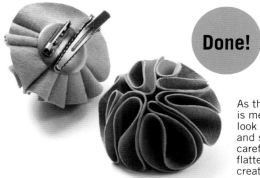

10 Super glue is applied for attaching the brooch pin/clip combo.

Done!

As this charm is meant to look light and soft, be careful not to flatten it when creating it.

VARIATION: SPHERICAL VERSION

1 We'll create a sphere using 12 folded discs. You'll have to follow Steps 1 to 6, but make bundles of 3 on the cord.

2 Just like in the picture, cross the cord once and pass the extremity underneath the loop.

3 If you make a knot with the two ends and tighten it, you will have a pom-pom! Pass a ball chain through it to create an accessory.

You could use it as an ornament and attach it to the tote bag on page 136.

Done!

72

Flower Charm

The flower petals will become three dimensional with heat and placed one on top of the other. The leather stamens and pistil will be the icing on the cake.

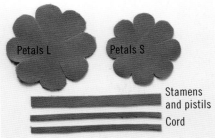

Petals L   Petals S

Stamens and pistils

Cord

1 Make a dent every two leaves to create the large petals of this flower. It should look like a four-leaf clover. The core of the flower will be created with one large strip, while the cord will be made out of two thinner strips.

2 As the flowers have a complicated figure, simply cut them out with scissors.

3 Open a hole with a ⁵⁄₃₂" dia (3.6mm) drive punch tool in the center of the two flowers.

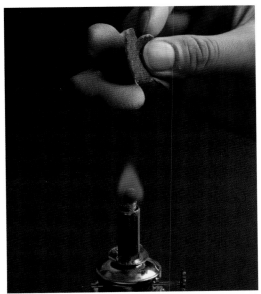

4 Move the edges of the flesh side of the petals over the fire, taking care not to burn the leather or yourself. The leather will shrink and take shape in the heat. Before starting, make sure you practice on scraps of leather.

5 The two flower parts should have this shape. If you are using a lighter, take extra care not to burn yourself.

6 Take the larger strip to make the center of the flower and cut fringes, leaving a 1/16" to 1/8" (2 to 3mm) upper strip for the glue. The shreds should be approximately 1/16" (2mm) wide.

7 Roll it once around one of the thinner strips and mark it when it becomes too thick. File its flesh side up to this mark.

8 Apply some contact cement on both sides of the unfringed strip but leave out the smooth bit on the grain side. Wait the required time.

9 Fix one cord on the edge of the fringed strip, flesh side against flesh side. File the grain-side tip of the cord for the glue.

10 Starting with that end, tightly roll the fringed strip around the cord and press it with something hard, like a wooden mallet.

11 Cut the tip of the cord as thinly as the fringes to camouflage it.

12 Pass the cord through the petals that you will have put on top of each other.

13 To fix the petals together, put some flex glue in one point and glue them together.

14 Completely pull down the cord through the petals to piece together the flower.

15 Make a loop with that cord and glue it together with some flex glue. Do the same with the other cord, slightly out of line from the other one.

16 Fix the flower on the brooch pin/clip with contact cement—and voilà! To create an accessory for your hair, just glue the elastic between the flower and a small leather disc.

Done!

When gluing it on the pin, apply some pressure but take care not to flatten the flower.

A four-stringed
Wallet Cord

This is a wallet cord braided with four strings. Both ends of the round braid will be attached to a lobster claw hook. You can create it either one- or two-toned and braid it any length you want.

Hint

The size and look of the braid will change with the strength used when braiding it. We usually braid it quite tightly, but this also depends on the type of leather.

Crafter: Tomoaki Motoyama

WHAT YOU'LL NEED
- Lacing awl
- Perma-lok lacing needle (big)

LEATHER USED
- Saddle lace: 1/16" (1.7mm) thickness; 5/32" (4mm) width; 70" (180cm) length (×2)

The round braid will be done by hand, but a perma-lok needle will be needed to close the braid. A lacing awl will help add convenience.

▶ Braiding the rope

1 Pass the two strands through the hook. We changed the colors of the strings to make this tutorial easier to understand.

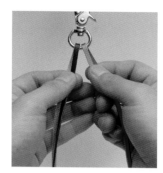

2 The brown and pink strands are in the front, while the green strand is behind the pink one and the beige is behind the brown one.

3 First, cross the two middle strands, bringing the brown in front.

4 Then, take the beige strand behind and bring it over between the brown and green strands and back to the left.

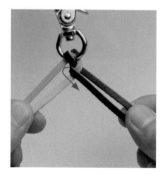

5 Do the same with the green, passing it behind and bringing it between the pink and beige strands and back to the right.

6 Bring the left outer strand (pink) around the back, over between the green and brown strands, and back to the left.

7 Bring the right outer strand (brown) around the back, over between the pink and beige strands, and back to the right. This is the same as Step 3.

8 Simply repeat Steps 4 to 7 until the round braid is the desired length.

▶ Closing the braid with a square stitch

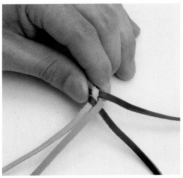

1 To end the wallet cord, have your round braid in the previous Step 6 position. Make sure the strands are tight.

2 If you turn it upside down, it will look like this.

3 Pass the beige strand over the green.

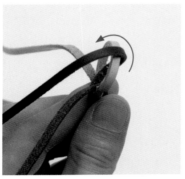

4 Pass the green strand over the beige.

5 Pass the pink strand over the green.

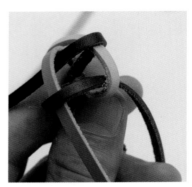

6 Pass the brown strand over the pink one and under the beige one.

7 Tighten all the strands equally. This is how the square stitch should look.

8 To insert the strands in the perma-lok needle, taper the tip with scissors.

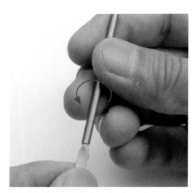

9 Starting with the beige strand, insert it in the needle and, turning the needle clockwise, push it down until it is tight.

10 Take the beige strand under where the pink and green strands cross and pull it out from the middle.

11 Take the green strand under where the brown and pink strands cross and pull it out from the middle.

12 Do the same with the pink strand where the beige and brown cross.

13 And do the same with the brown strand where the green and beige cross.

14 If you pull all the strands, it should look like this: four leather strings coming out from the middle part of the rope.

▶ Attaching the end of the rope to the other hook

1 Pass the beige strand in the hook.

2 With the perma-lok needle, pass the strand by its base and through the other side, like in the right-hand picture.

3 If you pull the beige strand, the hook will be in this position.

4 Pass the green strand through the hook.

5 Pass the strand by its base and pull it through the other side, like in the right-hand picture.

6 Pass the brown strand through the hook.

7 Pass it where the brown, green, and pink strands form a mesh and pull it through next to the beige strand.

8 This is how it should look. In the hook, the brown strand will be over the beige one.

9 Pass the pink strand through the hook.

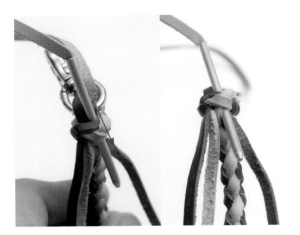

10 Pass it where the pink, beige, and brown strands form a mesh. Pull it through next to the green strand.

11 Tighten the mesh. The strands are now fastened to both hooks.

12 Cut the loose strands to your desired length. They look good if the strands are slightly shorter than the strand folded in two.

13 Trim the points to a sharp end. The sharper they are, the more stylish they will look.

Done!

Usually wallet cords are braided in one color, but it is easier to make mistakes that way. It is important that you are patient with this project.

Desk Tray
made with stacked leather

We are using the technique of "stacked leather" to create this stylish tray. It can be used for your glasses, watch, accessories, phone, and many other things.

Hint

This tray highlights the cut edges of the leather. It is thus important to carefully finish the edges, as their quality will reflect the overall quality of the finished product. If you want to dye the edges, choose a color paler than the leather.

WHAT YOU'LL NEED
- Small sanding pad with handle (1)
- Heavy canvas (2)
- Smoothing plane (3)
- Craft dye (orange) (4)
- 5 Compass (or divider caliper) (5)

LEATHER USED
- Aniline-finish cowhide
- ³⁄₃₂" (2mm) thick

1. To sand larger surfaces and curved surfaces. Convenient if you want to save time and increase your efficiency.
2. To smooth and polish the edges well. This cloth is easy to use.
3. To give a smooth surface to the stacked blocks of leather.
4. For dyeing the cut edges the same color as the leather.
5. Used to mark out the leather and measure distances.

Crafter: Ikkei Kobayashi   ▶ Pattern paper: page 167

1 To have an even surface when stacking the leather, cut the leather as straight as possible.

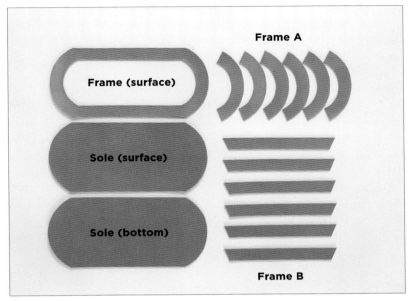

Frame A

Frame (surface)

Sole (surface)

Sole (bottom)

Frame B

2 Cut out 6 A and B pieces. We will stack them in three and then paste them on the loop—Frame (surface). A and B are in pieces to save leather when cutting them out. You can choose how many layers you want for A and B. The two sole pieces will be glued flesh side to flesh side.

3 With the Frame (surface) paper pattern, cut the sides of the inside of the frame, leaving uncut the straight bit. When you trace this shape on the leather, use a ruler to make a straight line.

4 Before stacking up the As and Bs, file all the grain sides.

5 Stack the As and Bs together, three at a time, with some flex glue. Be careful to always glue them with the grain side up.

6 When stacking the leather, carefully align the edges together. Press them together well by hammering the leather with a wooden mallet. With a plastic bone folder, remove any trapped air or excess glue by rubbing the leather outward.

7 You should end up with four pieces with three leather layers.

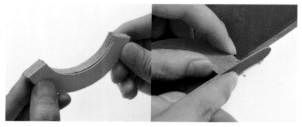

8 Check against the paper patterns that all the edges of the pieces match when attached together. If they don't, sand the excess down with a sanding stick.

9 Check with the Frame (surface) that the pieces fit well together.

10 First, glue the curved parts (pieces A) on the frame by applying flex glue on both the flesh side of the frame and the surface of the pieces.

11 Proceed by gluing the straight parts (pieces B) with the frame. Don't forget to glue the edges of pieces A and B together!

12 Once you have checked that there is no space between the parts, gently hammer the pieces together with a wooden mallet. This will ease filing the bottom of the loop.

13 With a sanding stick, finish off the edges of the loop. This must be done now, otherwise it will be too late.

TIP

Using a small triangular-shaped sanding pad will increase the speed of your work.

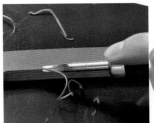 

14 Bevel the edges. With a sanding stick, file the edges once again to make them smoother.

15 Dye the inside with craft dye. Try to apply it as smoothly as possible.

16 Once done, apply glossing polish and polish it little by little, meticulously.

17 Try to polish the curved edges with heavy canvas; it will be much easier than with the plastic bone folder. If you do it vigorously, the leather will start to shine.

18 The inner edges have been finished. You will not be able to polish them later, so make sure that they are the way you want them.

19 Apply flex glue on the flesh sides of both soles and glue them together in a perfect fit.

20 Hammer it with a wooden mallet to harden the surface.

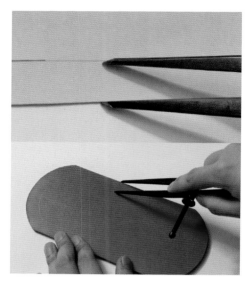

21 Measure the width of the loop with the paper pattern and compass. Make it ½₂" (1mm) shorter. Now, trace the width with the compass on the surface of the sole. This is where you will apply glue for the loop.

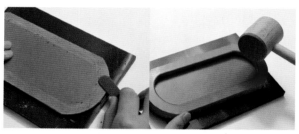

22 File the frame that you have just traced, apply glue on both the frame and the bottom of the loop, stick them together, and finally hammer the tray with a wooden mallet.

23 Make sure the loop and the base are aligned well, and sand down any irregularity.

TIP

With a smoothing plane, you can plane the edges off, and the finish it gives will be superior to the sanding stick or canvas. It is not an indispensible tool but a useful one nonetheless.

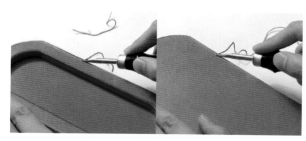

24 Bevel all the edges of the tray.

25 Sand down the edges and the beveled edges with a sanding stick.

26 Smoothly apply the craft dye on the outer edges, too.

27 To finish, apply the glossing polish and rub with a plastic bone folder. Control your strength, as the edges can tear apart if you rub too hard.

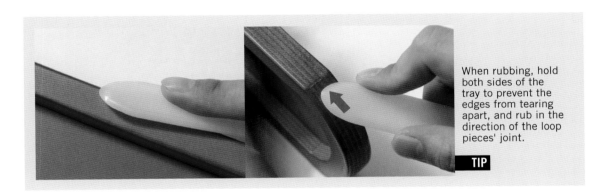

When rubbing, hold both sides of the tray to prevent the edges from tearing apart, and rub in the direction of the loop pieces' joint.

TIP

Done!

Refined and simple, this is an object that can be used in many different ways.

Elasticize leather to create a
Dinosaur Mobile

Vegetable-tanned leather is elastic by nature. Just like clay, once it is wet you will be able to mold it into almost anything, and once dry it will keep its new shape. You will be able to work on the leather as long as you keep it humid, so take your time and try out this new technique!

Hint

As an alternative, you can use colored leather to create more creatures. And you do not necessarily need to use them on a mobile to make a good impression!

WHAT YOU'LL NEED
- Scissors—To cut out the complex patterns
- Cable cutter—Used when cutting the copper cable for the mobile.

LEATHER USED
- Cowhide ¹⁄₁₆" (1.5mm) thick leather patterns

If you are making the mobile, use a 3/32" (2mm) copper wire and some nylon thread.

Crafter: Tomoaki Motoyama
▶ Pattern paper: pages 174–175

▶ Cutting the patterns and shaping the head

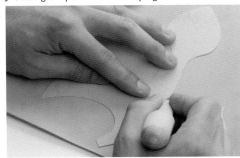

Pteranodon

The hardest part is the head, so work carefully on it. The wings will come to life once you have folded them slightly. But the overall impression will all depend on how balanced you have shaped your dinosaur.

1 Trace the patterns with a round awl on the grain side.

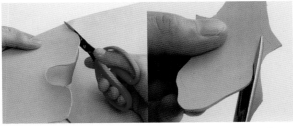

2 Cut the head pattern with scissors, first roughly and then more precisely.

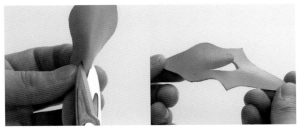

3 Once you have cut out the head, fold it lengthwise and make a small cut on the top of the head.

4 Cut out the body pattern, too.

5 Open the eyes with a ⅛" dia (3.0mm) punch drive tool.

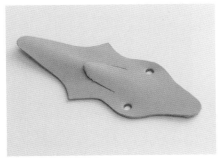

6 This is how the head should look. We will now start to shape it.

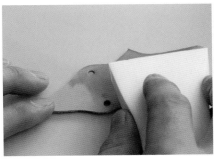

7 Wet the flesh side of the head two or three times.

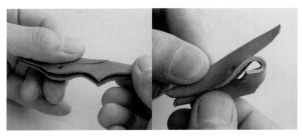

8 Once you have soaked it in water, fold the head lengthwise and bring the lower jaw under the upper jaw. Make sure the upper jaw is slightly protruding.

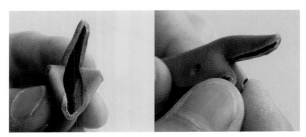

9 Keep the jaws in place and press both hinges together, just like in the picture.

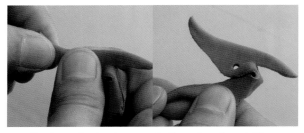

10 To shape the beak, curve both ends outward. You should pinch the beak and pull it toward the outside.

11 Give the head a three-dimensional form by expanding the back of the jaw. If the leather is dry, wet it again.

12 Reshape the head until you are satisfied with its balance, and let it completely dry.

▶ Shaping the body

1 Soak the flesh side of the body two or three times.

2 Fold the leather lengthwise to create the crease of the backbone.

3 Make a mountain-shaped crease where the collarbone should be, perpendicular to the backbone.

4 Roll the legs outward but leave the feet stretched.

5 Fold the foremost edge of the wings.

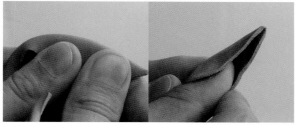

6 Pinch the belly and curve it, then give it some swelling by pushing its lining toward the outside.

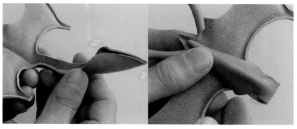

7 Fold the belly under the back of the dinosaur. The end of the belly should be placed halfway over the tail.

8 Pinch and fit the top and bottom parts of the neck together until the chest and belly fit snugly under the back of the dinosaur.

9 Check that the upper and lower parts of the collarbone are aligned by reshaping the creases of the back.

10 Fold the edges of the wings again, and bend the tips downward.

11 Fold the feet upside down and arrange the shape of the wings to your liking.

12 Cut the claws with scissors: 3 for the front feet and 4 for the rear feet.

▶ Attaching the head to the body

1 Once both parts have dried, sand a ³⁄₁₆" (5mm) border on the grain side of the chest and belly. Apply flex glue and glue the front and back parts of the body together.

2 Position the two parts together and mark the part of the body that will be glued. With a sanding stick, abrade that part.

3 Abrade the inside of the head and apply flex glue.

4 Apply flex glue on the abraded portion of the body, and glue the two parts together.

Done!

Created with very little leather and basic tools, this dinosaur is nonetheless sturdy.

> ▶ Shaping the head

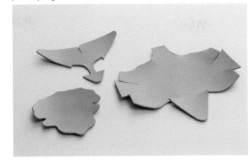

1 Cut out the shapes of the triceratops.

Triceratops

The triceratops' head is created with two pieces, the horns and the face. The horns and frills (the cartilaginous projection about the neck) need to be constantly wetted in order to shape them.

2 Open the holes for the eyes and horns. The upper horns will need an $^{11}/_{32}$" dia (9.0mm) punch drive tool, the lower fang a ¼" dia (6.0mm), and the eyes a ⅛" dia (3.0mm).

3 This is how it should look.

4 Soak the flesh side of the face two or three times with water.

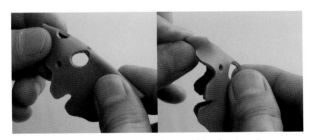

5 Make a middle crease, leaving out the forehead. To create the beak, pinch and pull the tip of the face downward.

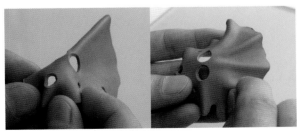

6 Fold the cheeks slightly to give the face a three-dimensional look. Then start folding the frills of the animal into pleats.

7 The head will look like this.

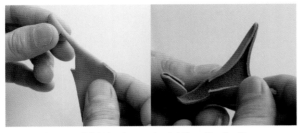

8 We will now fold the horns by folding the leather lengthwise and rounding the three horns like a cone.

9 It will look like this.

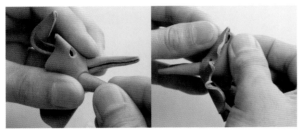

10 When fitting the two pieces together, the fang should be protruding from the face by ¹³⁄₃₂" (1cm), while the horn will be 1 ³⁄₁₆" (3cm).

11 Bend the horns forward while rolling them.

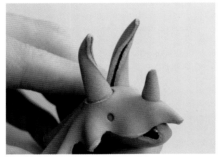

12 The horns should look like this.

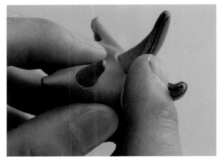

13 Hold the head by the sides and try to flatten the forehead.

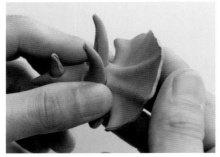

14 Hold the sides of the horns and head and open up the frills until the head has a good balance to it.

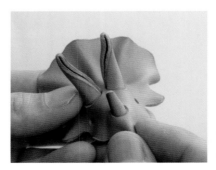

15 Rearrange the triceratops' head.

16 The head is now finished. Now dry it.

▶ Shaping the body

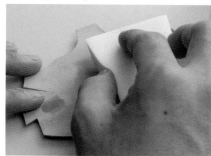

1 Wet the flesh side with water two or three times.

2 Fold it in two and create a curved spine by firmly pinching and pulling the leather.

3 Roll the tail into a cone.

4 Roll the four legs too.

5 Fold the edges of the belly inward at a right angle. The folded part should be ³⁄₁₆" (5mm) wide.

6 Slide your thumb under the belly and rub the leather to create a rounder belly.

7 Shape the legs so that the shoulders/ forelegs and bottom/hind legs have a natural shape.

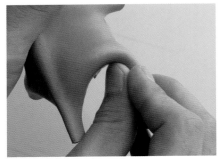

8 Bend the forelegs forward so that the shoulder/foreleg line is curved in a U shape.

9 Do the same with the rear legs and balance their shape with the forelegs.

10 Pinch the end of the neck and push it inward to create a bent neck. Once done, dry the body.

▶ Attaching the head to the body

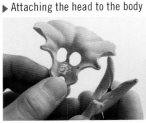

1 Disassemble the head and apply flex glue where the two touch each other. Glue the head together.

2 Abrade the folded ³⁄₁₆" (5mm) strip of the belly and apply flex glue to glue it together.

3 Abrade the tip of the neck and apply flex glue where the head and neck meet. Glue them together.

Done!

The head is quite heavy, but, because we have bent the forelegs, the triceratops should be able to stand up.

Creating a Dinosaur Mobile

We will create a mobile with the triceratops and pteranodon we have just made. As with most mobiles, it is important to achieve the right balance with the weights.

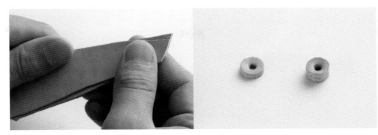

1 We will create two types of stoppers, the thicker one being made out of two layers of leather. Cut them both out with a ¼" dia (6.0mm) drive punch tool and pierce them with a ⅟₁₆" dia (1.2mm) one.

2 Tape the nylon thread to a point where the pteranodon will be stable.

3 Once you found your point, make a hole on the back of the dinosaur with a round awl and pass the thread through the back and then in between the layers with a needle.

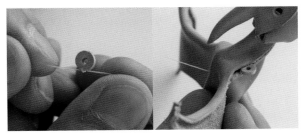

4 Tie a single-layer stopper to the belly-side end of the thread, and hide it in the lining.

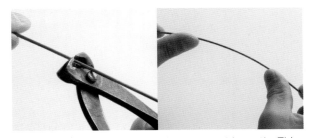

5 Cut the ³⁄₃₂" (2mm) copper wire and bend it gently. This time we are using 7 ½" (19cm) and 6 ¼" (16cm)-long wires.

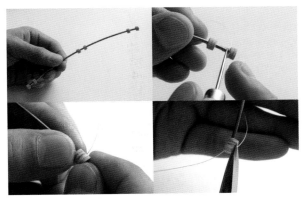

6 Prepare six thick stoppers and thread them on the wire. Glue the two beads at the extremities with flex glue. Attach the threads in between each couple of beads.

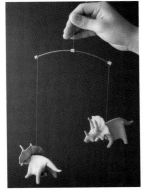

7 Hang the structure and see where the middle thread should go to give it equilibrium. Glue the middle stoppers once you have found balance.

Textured
Sheep Skull Necklace

This sheep skull was inspired by Native American art. We have used the elasticity of the leather to create a three-dimensional skull and have added texture with a modeling point. You can personalize it further with colorful leather beads.

Hint

Increase the authenticity of your skull by texturing it with a modeling point. Practice this beforehand on scraps of leather.

The techniques you will learn in this project can easily be used to create other items!

WHAT YOU'LL NEED
- Modeling tool point/ stylus—Used to add texture and create the main characteristic of this skull. Has two different tips.
- Leather hardener—An agent used to stiffen the leather to keep its shape.
- Craft dye—To dye the leather beads. Use your preferred colors.
- Super glue—It is used when pasting metal fittings on lace.

LEATHER USED
- Cowhide ¹⁄₁₆" (1.5mm) thick

Crafter: Tomoaki Motoyama
▶ Paper pattern: page 172

▶ **CUTTING OUT THE PATTERNS AND OPENING HOLES**

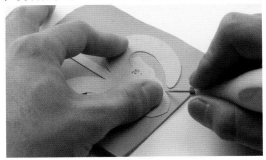

1 Trace the pattern onto the grain side of the leather.

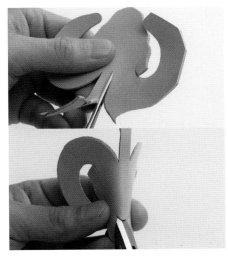

2 Cut it out with scissors. They are easier to use than a leather knife for finer details.

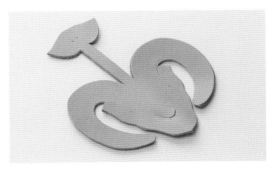

3 This is the cut-out leather. We will use the elasticity of the material to create a 3D shape.

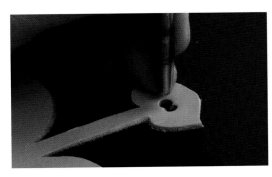

4 Open two holes close to each other at the back of the head with a ⅛" dia (3.0mm) drive punch tool. They will be used to fasten the skull to the necklace.

5 With scissors, cut out the excess leather between the two holes so that they become a single long hole.

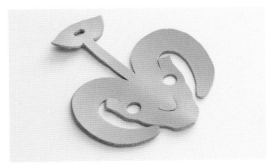

6 Open the eyes with a size 12 (7.5mm) drive punch tool.

▶ CREATING A THREE-DIMENSIONAL SKULL

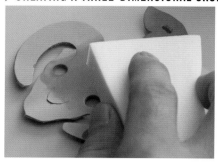

1 It is important to moisten or "case" well the leather with a wet sponge.

2 Mountain-fold the nose.

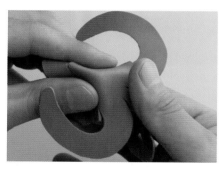

3 Pinch the two eyes together to create a triangular fold at the base of the forehead.

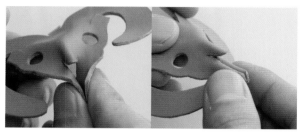

4 Valley-fold the chin and then mountain-fold the jaw's sides.

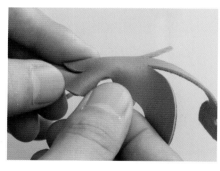

5 Make a faint diagonal mountain fold under the eyes.

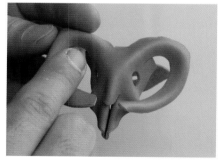

6 Bend the horns from the tip to the base. Start straight at the hairline, and then bend at an acute angle.

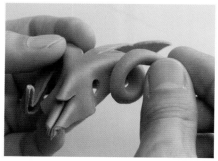

7 Continue to bend it until you achieve a curve similar to the one pictured.

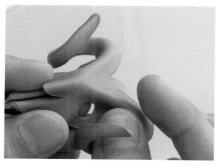

8 Remold the skull until you achieve the desired shape.

9 Fold the indented flaps. They will be glued later on.

10 Fold the prolonged part on the top of the head and pass it through the slit you made at the beginning.

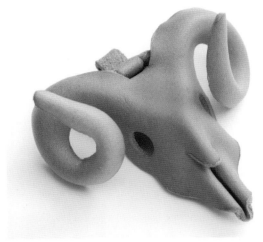

11 Look at your skull from different angles and adjust its shape accordingly.

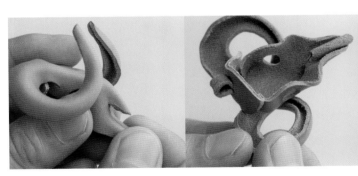

12 Firm the structure of the skull, with the nose lengthening downward and the upper jaws upward.

13 Fold the top part of the head so that it is aligned with the indented flaps.

14 Round the eye sockets with a pen. The eyes will look more real if their lower edges are more sunken in than the upper edges.

15 We will add texture to the head once you have shaped it.

▶ ADDING TEXTURE FOR A LIFELIKE SKULL

1 Using these pictures as a model, add sinews to the skull with a modeling point.

2 We have created cracks in the skull.

3 To create the ridges in the horns, start by indenting the bases with a downward curve.

4 Continue to carve the ridges with thin and tight dents that go from one side of the horn to the other.

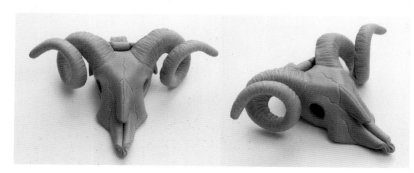

5 Once you have added texture to the skull, dry the leather thoroughly.

▶ **FINISHING UP**

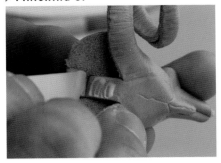

1 Once dry, apply glue on the back of the skull and the two indented flaps.

2 Glue them together.

3 Make sure they are firmly glued.

4 Apply the leather hardener. Normally it is used on the flesh side only, but for this item we will apply it on both sides.

5 Your sheep skull pendant is ready once the hardener has dried.

▶ **MAKING LEATHER BEADS**

1 Punch ³⁄₃₂" (2mm)- and ⅛" (3mm)-thick vegetable-tanned cowhide leather with an ¹¹⁄₃₂" dia (9.0mm) punch drive tool.

2 Make a hole in the middle of these bits with a ³⁄₁₆" dia (4.5mm) drive tool.

3 Put the dye in a small container and dip the beads to dye them. You can choose any color, and the more the better.

4 Dry them once you have dyed them.

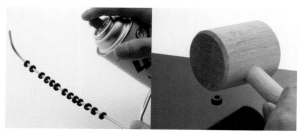

5 Coat them with a leather spray lacquer and gently flatten them with the side of a wooden mallet.

6 Combine the colors of your choice.

7 Cut an 18" (46cm)-long, ⁵⁄₃₂" (4mm)-round cow leather string. Thread the beads and the pendant.

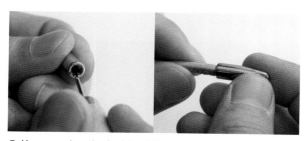

8 You can glue the inside of the clasps with the ends of the string.

Done!

The necklace is finished once the glue has dried. You can also create a bracelet with only leather beads.

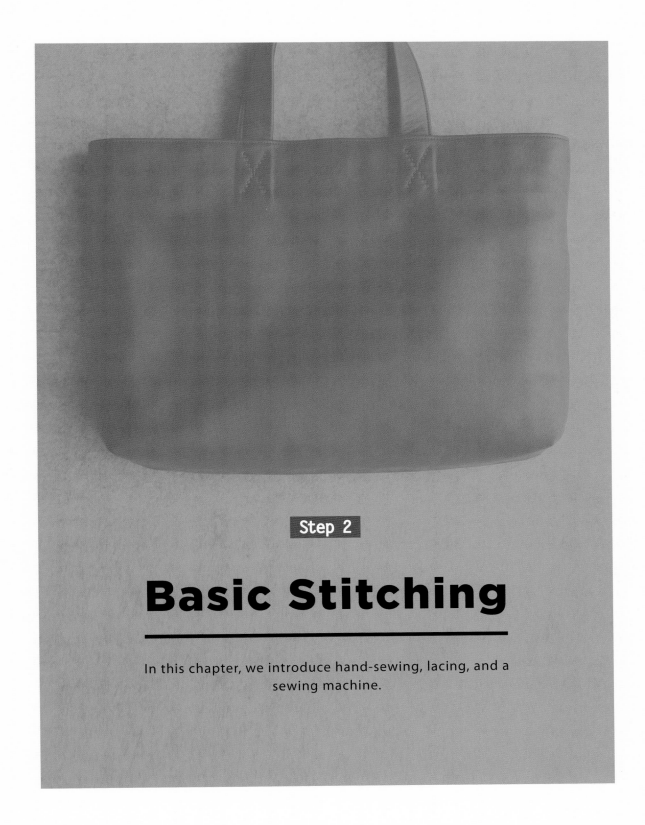

Step 2

Basic Stitching

In this chapter, we introduce hand-sewing, lacing, and a sewing machine.

Tools Used in Step 2

In this section, we will start to stitch leather items.

When hand-sewing leather, you will of course use needles and threads. Unlike cloth, leather will have to be pierced with a diamond-shaped thonging chisel before you pull the needle through it.

You will also need to punch holes before you start lacing leather, but this can be done with a chisel for slits, or a round awl for round holes. A finely pointed needle will have to be used for the stitching. There are many lacing techniques, but in Step 2 we will be using the simple running stitch.

With a sewing machine, you won't need to open holes beforehand. Using a machine will also considerably shorten the time spent on sewing. However, all the items that can be made with the machine can also be sewn by hand.

The tools used in steps 2 and 3 are the same.

THINGS YOU'LL NEED TO PUNCH SEWING HOLES

As a standard, sewing holes need to be opened with a thonging chisel. But for uneven surfaces or edges and finer points, we suggest using a round awl. To mark the sewing line on leather ⅟₁₆" (1.5mm) thick or thinner, you will need to use either a plastic bone folder or a divider. For leather thicker than ⅟₁₆" (1.6mm+), use a stitching groover.

Thonging chisels
With a two-pronged and a four-pronged chisel, which have different spacing, you should be able to create most items.

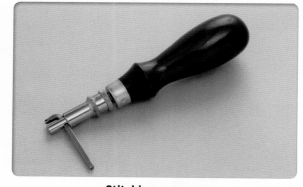

Stitching groover
It is used on thicker leather to draw the groove along which you will sew. It will serve as a guide and make your stitching look even.

Round awl, Rubber mat, and Felt
These items are used in the same way as in Step 1. The round awl is useful for opening delicate sewing holes or marking reference points. The rubber mat and felt need to be used when hammering the thonging chisel.

THINGS YOU'LL NEED TO HAND-SEW

Unlike cloth-sewing, you will need to wax your thread before you start sewing leather. Linen thread and the beeswax with which you'll wax your thread are usually included in the starter's kits, but there are other alternatives. You can buy already-waxed thread, as well as nylon and polyester threads, in specialty stores.

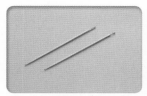

Hand-sewing needles
There are many kinds of needles you could use, but the ones included in the basic kits are generally thin and blunt. You should match the size of the needle with the thickness of the thread.

Linen thread (medium)
This thread needs to be waxed before use, but the natural fiber will make your hand-sewing stand out.

Beeswax
Waxing the thread makes it stronger and prevents it from unraveling when sewing.

THINGS YOU'LL NEED TO LACE

You will need to choose the chisel according to the width of the stitching space of your project. We recommend you use the round awl no.8 for running stitches. There are many types of needles you could use, so chose one you would feel comfortable with.

Chisel
To punch slits in the leather, through which you will pass the lace. There are chisels with ³⁄₃₂" (2mm) and ⅛" (3mm) spacing. Choose the one that will fit your lace best.

Lacing needle/ Lacing awl
The needle for lacing, attached at the tip of a lace, and the awl for pushing the lace.

SEWING MACHINE

A sewing machine will dramatically decrease the time spent on sewing leather. It will also allow you to create a wider range of items. However, you will need a heavy-duty machine to machine-sew leather. Please check first if your sewing machine is compatible with leather crafting.

Home leather 110
The heavy-duty sewing machine that can sew leather for home use. ⁵⁄₃₂" (4.5mm)-thick tannin leather can be sewn.

Hand-sewn leather
Key Cover

This key cover is created by simply sewing together the edges. As it requires very little sewing, this project is particularly suited for beginners. The sewing patterns come into two different sizes to fit the most common key blanks, but it is easy to alter the shape and customize your key cover.

Hint

If the cover is too large, it will be difficult to fit the key cover hole with the key hole. Check your keys against the patterns.

If you decide to customize the key cover, make sure that it will fit your key. This product can be made with a basic tool box.

WHAT YOU'LL NEED
- It should all be included in the starter's kit.

LEATHER USED
- Barchetta leather ¹⁄₁₆" (1.7 mm) thick

Crafter: Tomoaki Motoyama
▸ Paper pattern: page 166

▶ How to cut the pattern and punch a hole

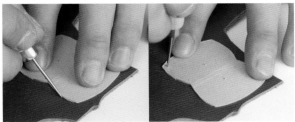

1 Use a round awl to trace the contours of the paper pattern onto the grain side. Then make small perforations to mark the center of the key hole and where the seams start and end.

2 With a leather knife, cut into the leather along the traced pattern.

3 File and even the edges with a sanding stick where the key is inserted.

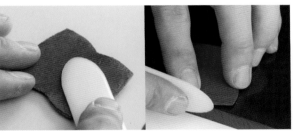

4 With some glossing polish, paint and polish the flesh side and the edges that will be sewn together.

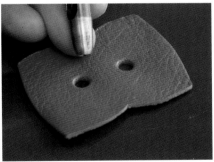

5 Use a ³⁄₁₆" dia (4.5mm) leather drive punch tool to punch the holes. Make sure that the holes are lined up when the leather is folded over.

6 To glue the leather together, smooth out the margins of the flesh side with a sanding stick.

7 Apply a thin coat of flex glue on the filed margins.

8 Fold the leather in two and paste it together before the glue dries.

▶ Sewing

1 Once the piece is glued, smooth the edges with a sanding stick once again.

2 After the sanding is done, mark the lines along which you will sew, ⅛" (3mm) away from the edges.

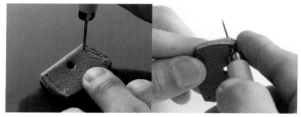

3 With the round awl, perforate the four points which will mark the start and the end of the sewing lines.

4 Use a thonging chisel to make holes along the sewing lines, starting and finishing with the pin-pricked holes.

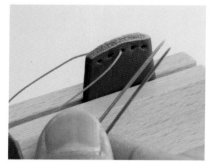

5 Start by pulling the needle through the third hole until you are at the center of the thread. The key cover will be backstitched.

6 Hand stitch in one direction.

7 Repeat the previous step until you reach the end and then start backstitching.

8 Cut the thread close to the leather.

9 To even out the edges, cut the excess leather.

10 Pass over the edges with a sanding stick.

11 Coat the key cover with glossing polish and finish off the cut edges with a plastic bone folder.

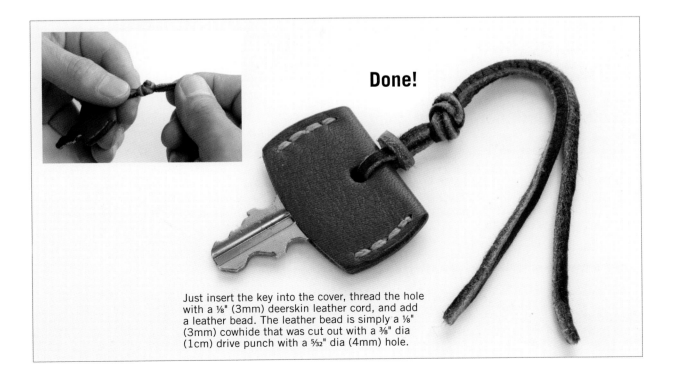

Done!

Just insert the key into the cover, thread the hole with a ⅛" (3mm) deerskin leather cord, and add a leather bead. The leather bead is simply a ⅛" (3mm) cowhide that was cut out with a ⅜" dia (1cm) drive punch with a ⁵⁄₃₂" dia (4mm) hole.

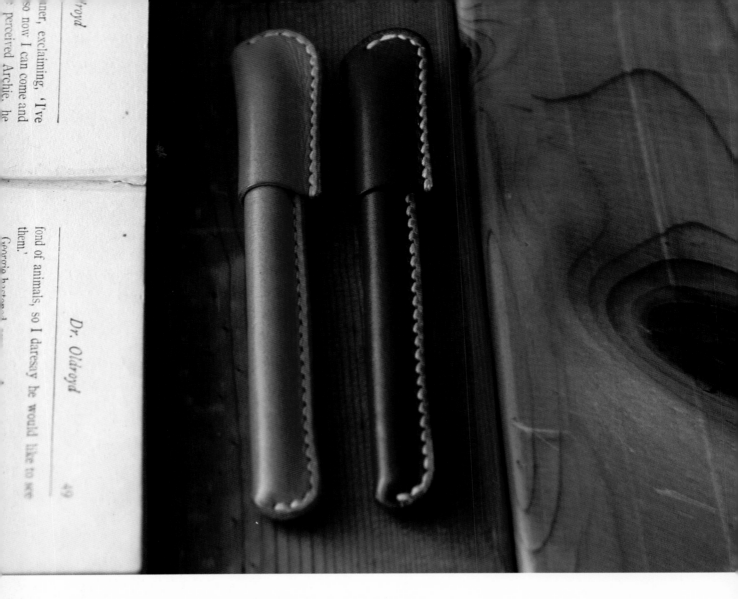

Learning the basics of hand stitching for a
Pen Cover

By merely covering a plastic pen with it, it has the power to change the look of your desk. We will be sewing in a straight line, but the case will have to be rounded in order to insert the pen. Once you will have created this, you will be able to make more complicated designs involving stitching. This cover has been created for a 5⁄16″ (8mm) pen.

Hint
Although very simple to make, the leather will mold to your hand's shape, making it easier to write, and will give a luxurious feel to the cheapest plastic pens.

WHAT YOU'LL NEED
It should all be included in the starter's kit.

LEATHER USED
• Cowhide 1⁄16" (1.3mm) thick

Crafter: Tomoaki Motoyama
▶ Paper pattern: page 171

▶ Cutting and gluing the patterns

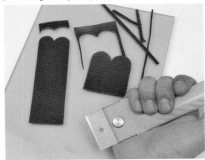

1 Cut the patterns according to the paper pattern.

2 When hand stitching, we will mark the stitches' holes with a round awl.

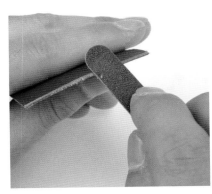

3 We will first finish the opening of the cap cover. File the cut edges with a sanding stick, and apply some glossing polish.

4 Apply polish on the flesh side of the cap and rub with a bone folder until it is smooth and slick.

5 File a margin of ⅛" (3mm) on the flesh side. We will later apply glue to it.

6 File a similar margin on the body of the pen cover.

7 Apply flex glue on the filed margins.

8 Fold them in two and apply pressure on the glued part with the bone folder.

9 Once the glue is dry, file the edges with a sanding stick.

▶ Stitching

1 On a rubber mat, mark the last stitching point with a round awl.

2 From there to the opening of the cap cover, mark the stitching line.

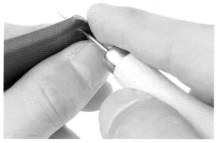

3 Open the last stitching point with the round awl.

4 Starting from that point, open the rest of the stitching holes with a thonging chisel. Use a two-pronged one for the curved part.

5 We will start stitching the cap cover. Make sure you stitch the first and last part of the running stitch twice.

6 This is how it should look. File the cut margins again.

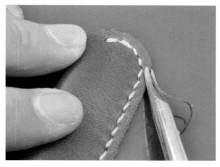

7 Bevel the edges that have been stitched together.

8 File the beveled edges once again and apply glossing polish on it, then rub to bring the shine out.

9 Go through the same steps with the body of the pen cover.

10 Insert the pen in the finished cover.

11 Fully insert the pen and mold the cover until it has a flattering shape.

Done!

This is a leather pen cover that will become easier to use as time goes by.

12 Cover it with the cap and shape it until you are satisfied with its form.

Business Card Holder

This is a perfect piece to practice your stitching on! The deerskin braid, thick thread, and small silver concha lend it an ethnic flair. Made with vegetable-tanned leather, you will also be able to enjoy the aging patina of this card holder.

Hint

To go with the thicker thread used in this project, use a wide-spaced thonging chisel. If you want to change the weight of the thread, make sure you are using the right thonging chisel. You can also try to enrich it with ornamental techniques that are shown in the Decorative Techniques section.

Crafter: Ikkei Kobayashi

WHAT YOU'LL NEED

- Compass (or divider caliper)
- Standard tool for tracing the stitching line. You can also use a plastic bone folder.
- Glass slicker to polish the linings.
- Thick waxed synthetic thread
- Robust polyester that has already been waxed and is ready for use.

LEATHER USED

- Body: vegetable-tanned leather ⅛" (2.5mm) thick
- Pockets: vegetable-tanned leather ¹⁄₁₆" (1.5mm) thick

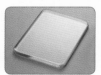

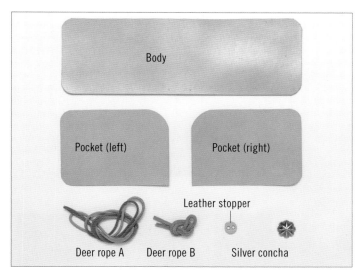

Body

Pocket (left)

Pocket (right)

Leather stopper

Deer rope A   Deer rope B   Silver concha

1 Choose the right leather for the body and pockets of the card holder (as detailed in the "Choosing your leather section" sidebar on page 15). Looking at the image, the grain flow should be horizontal for the pockets but vertical for the body. The deer rope should be ³⁄₃₂" (2mm) wide and 35" (90cm) long for A, and ⅛" (3mm) wide and 6" (15cm) long for B.

2 Create the leather stopper with a ½" dia (12mm) and a ⅛" dia (3.0mm) drive punch tool.

3 We will use a ²⁵⁄₃₂" (2cm)-wide silver concha for this project.

4 Bevel both sides of the leather and finely sand down the edges. The end result should look like the picture on the right.

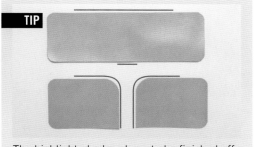

TIP

The highlighted edges have to be finished off now, as you won't be able to do them later.

5 Uniformly apply glossing polish on the flesh sides of the pieces and rub it in with a plastic bone folder until the leather becomes smooth. Take care not to smudge the grain side, as stains will remain.

TIP

To finish off large sections of leather, use a glass trowel to speed up and increase the quality of your craft.

6 Finish off the edges with the glossing polish in the same manner.

7 Once you have marked the position of the holes with the paper pattern, open the rope hole with a 9/64" dia (3.6mm) drive punch tool and the concha hole with a 3/16" dia (4.5mm).

8 Cut rope A in three equal parts, knot one end, clip to one place, and braid them with the flesh side facing up.

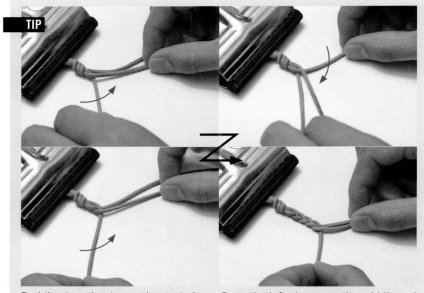

TIP

Braiding is a simple weaving technique. Cross the left piece over the middle and then cross the right piece over the middle. Continue crossing the left and right piece over the middle and keep the flesh side facing up.

9 Once you have woven a 4" (10cm) braid, make a knot like in the picture to secure it.

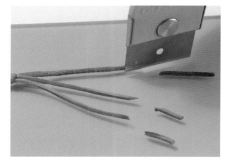

10 Cut the strands to an appropriate length. The braid will look good if cut slightly slanted.

11 The braid will be used to tie the card holder together. We will now pass it into its hole.

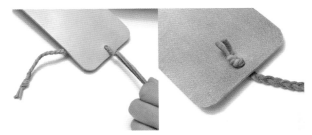

12 Thread the hole like in the picture. The first knot of the braid should be bigger than the hole.

13 Thread rope B with the concha and pass it through the other hole. Secure it on the flesh side with the stopper.

14 Check first how loose the concha should be to tie the braid around it.

15 Knot the lace in that position and cut the strands, leaving roughly ¾6" (5mm) ends.

16 Fix the knot with some flex glue.

17 As glue cannot easily be applied to polished leather, sand down a ¾6" (5mm) margin on the sides to be stitched. Apply flex glue.

18 Glue the pockets and the body together well by rubbing them.

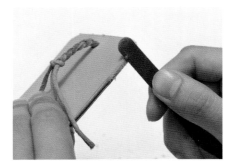

19 Finish off the glued edges with a sanding stick.

20 Use the plastic bone folder as shown to mark the stitching line on the inside of the card holder.

TIP

If you are using a compass, make sure to adjust the stitching line to ⅛" (3mm) from the edges.

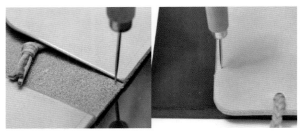

21 Open the four start and end stitches with a round awl. As shown, the two bottom holes should only go through the main body of the card holder.

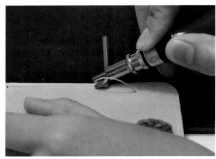

22 Make a groove ⅛" (3mm) from the edge with the adjustable stitching groover. (If you are working on thinner leather, use a compass.)

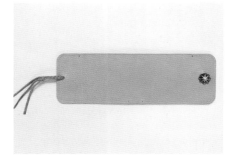

23 We have created grooves to facilitate stitching. Before marking the card holder, practice grooving on scraps of leather.

24 Open the holes and sew. Take care not to sew the thread.

25 Bevel both sides of the stitched corners.

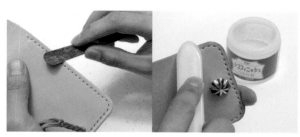

27 Slide a plastic bone folder into the pockets and push it close to the stitches to start breaking in the leather.

26 Using the finer grit side of the sanding stick, sand down all the stitched edges and rub on glossing polish.

Done!

Your card holder is finished after you have created space to store business cards. Ensure that you have smoothed out any fuzziness before starting the stitching process.

Leather-lined
Pen Case

This pen case was created by lining a vegetable-tanned cowhide with thinned pigskin. Lining this item gives a much more professional finish than simply polishing the flesh side of the cowhide. The leather belt is also another simple but classy feature of this pen case. This can be created in the colors of your choice.

Hint
The final look of this pen case will depend a lot on the leather used to line it. You can try to combine different types of leather and colors and use any type of leather thinner than ⅟₃₂" (0.5mm) to line this.

WHAT YOU'LL NEED
● It should all be included in the starter's kit.

LEATHER USED
● Body: Cowhide ⅟₁₆" (1.3mm) thick
● Lining: Pigskin lining leather ⅟₆₄" (0.5mm) thick

Crafter: Tomoaki Motoyama

▶ Cutting the pieces and lining

1 Place the paper patterns on the leather and cut the pieces, but cut the belt and linings of Part A a little bigger than their patterns. We will cut them again once they are glued to the main parts.

2 Apply flex glue on the flesh side of the belt and its lining hide and glue them together.

▶ Bend-gluing the pen case flap

1 When lining Part A, bend the fold of the flap 90° while gluing it.

2 Cut the lining that sticks out from Part A.

3 We will line only the central part of Part B. With a round awl, mark the section that will be lined.

4 Apply flex glue on the section that will be lined, taking care not to spill out of the marks.

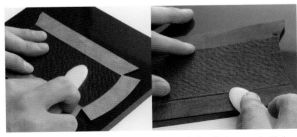

5 Apply flex glue on the flesh side of the lining and stick it to Part B. Use glossing polish to smooth out the non-lined parts.

6 This is how the leather should be lined, cut, and evened up.

▶ Finishing off the edges

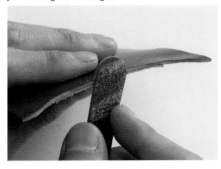

1 We will first sew the opening of Part B. To start with, smooth the cut edges with a sanding stick.

2 Trace the stitching line ⅛" (3mm) from the edges on Part B.

3 Mark the first and last stitches on the stitching line with a round awl.

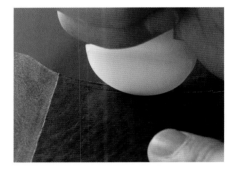

4 Trace the same stitching line on the lining.

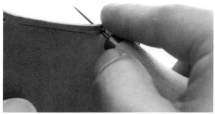

5 Completely open the first and last stitching holes with a round awl.

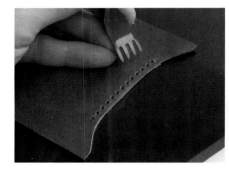

6 Open the stitching holes between the first and last holes with a thonging chisel.

7 Hand stitch with two needles, taking care to backstitch the first and last holes.

8 We will stitch the leather belt, too, so take a sanding stick and start smoothing its edges.

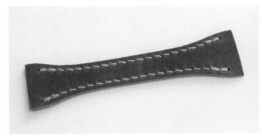

9 Stitch the belt like you just stitched Part B. Do not sew the sides, as these will be sewn later on the body.

10 Bevel the cut edges that you just stitched, and smooth them with a sanding stick.

11 You can now dye the stitched edges of Part B in the color of your choice and polish it with a glossing polish.

12 Do the same with the stitched edges of the leather belt.

▶ File the parts where the belt and Part B will be stitched

1 Take Part B, and with a sanding stick, file ⅛" (3mm) margins on all the edges that will later be stitched.

2 File the reverse side of the belt and the grain side of Part B where they will be stitched together.

3 The triangular indentation will become the gusset. Apply flex glue on its edges.

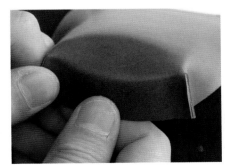

4 Create the gusset by sticking together the edges.

▶ Open the stitching holes with the round awl

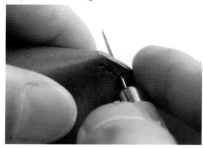

1 Create a stitching line on the gusset, and with the help of the paper pattern and a round awl, open three stitching holes.

2 The holes should be in the same position as in the picture.

3 Stitch the gusset. Start stitching from the central hole, stitch both sides twice, and end where you started off.

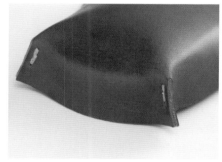

4 We have stitched both gussets.

5 Bevel and sand both sides.

6 After you have dyed the gusset's edges, apply glossing polish and finish them off.

▶ Gluing the main parts

1 Gently fold the creased parts of Part B inward. The fold should follow the shape of the lining.

2 Now fold the stitching line of Part B outward.

3 File the stitching edge of Part A and glue it on Part B. Try to align them perfectly.

4 Once you have glued them together, rub the edges with a bone folder.

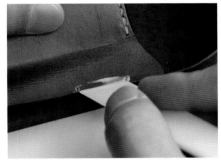

5 To glue the leather belt on the pen case, apply flex glue where the leather has been filed on both Part B and the belt.

6 Stick them together and rub with the bone folder.

7 The shape of the pen case was formed. The next step is begun after the glue has dried.

▶ Stitching and finishing off the pen case

1 File the glued edges with a sanding stick.

2 Mark the stitching line. You can do it with a bone folder, but it will be easier with a compass.

3 Mark the two corner stitching holes with the round awl. These holes should be in the creases of the gusset.

4 Create a stitching line on Part A, too. You can use the edges of the rubber mat as a support.

5 To mark the start and end stitches, make a hole where the different layers of leather meet.

6 Starting from one of the holes done with the round awl, open the stitching holes.

7 Double-stitch the leather belt and all the first and last stitching holes.

8 When stitching the corners, pass the needle in the middle of the gusset, where the edges meet.

9 The gussets will have to be sewn like in this picture. Make sure that they are well glued or you won't be able to properly stitch them.

10 Finish sewing by double-stitching the last hole.

11 The flap is sewn separately so that the stitches go in the same direction when it is folded over. Leave the space of one stitch between the seams of the flap and the body.

12 This is how the pen case should look once it is all sewn together. Make sure the first and last stitches of the flap are sewn twice.

13 Finish off the edges of the entire pen case. Bevel them and sand them.

14 Dye the edges and polish them with glossing polish.

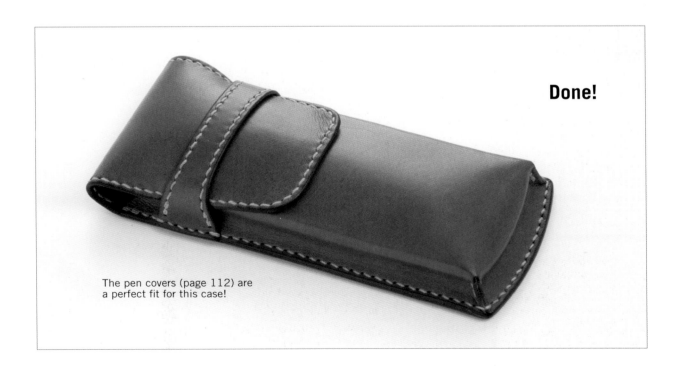

Done!

The pen covers (page 112) are a perfect fit for this case!

Card Holder

made with a running stitch

This card holder has a very soft and delicate look, with its round corners and deer leather stitches. But you can always make it more masculine by changing the leather and cord of the card holder. The two holes were created to allow you to know which card is in the card holder.

<table>
<tr>
<td>

Hint

You can change the colors of the leather and the cord to have a very unique card holder. It is not necessary to open the two "peep holes." You can either use the more elegant vegetable-tanned leather or softer chrome-tanned leather.

</td>
<td>

WHAT YOU'LL NEED
- Three ³⁄₃₂" dia (2.4mm) drive punch tools welded together. Not absolutely necessary, but very useful when you open the stitching holes.
- Compass—Used to mark the spaces between the stitches. You will need to measure the spacing against the paper pattern.

*Also prepare the tools used for lacing leather.

LEATHER USED
- Shrinking cowhide

Crafter: Megumi Hoshi
▶ Paper pattern: page 170

</td>
<td>

</td>
</tr>
</table>

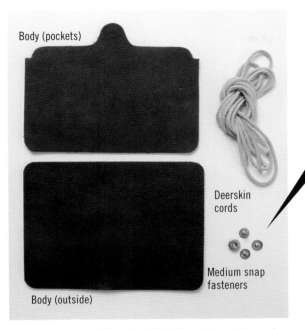

Body (pockets)

Deerskin cords

Medium snap fasteners

Body (outside)

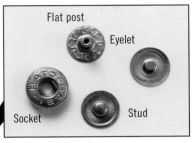

Flat post

Eyelet

Socket

Stud

One snap set is usually made of a snap cap, an eyelet, a socket, and a stud. In this case, though, to make the snap invisible we will use a flat post instead of a snap cap.

1 Prepare two ³⁄₃₂" (2mm) x 35" (90cm) deerskin cords and a set of medium snap fasteners.

TIP

The cap part on the right will be part of the standard cap set and the flat cap on the left is bought separately. Notice the difference in size.

2 Spread a thin coat of glossing polish on both flesh sides of the leather pieces and use a bone folder to rub it.

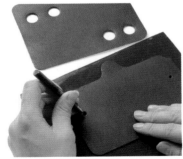

3 Determine the position of the holes on the leather pieces with the paper patterns. Open the bigger hole on Body (pockets) with a ³⁄₁₆" dia (4.5mm) drive punch tool, the small with a ³⁄₃₂" dia (2.4mm), and the big hole on Body (outside) with a ½" dia (15mm).

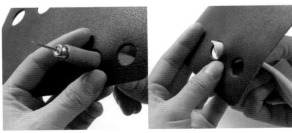

4 Finish off the edges of the peep holes now. Use the handle of the round awl or a heavy-duty cloth to do this.

5 Assemble the snap fasteners. The male part should go through the smaller hole and the female part in the bigger hole. Make sure that they close together on the grain side of the pockets.

6 There should not be any space between the snaps when they are riveted. If needed, use some leather padding in between.

TIP

The padding is made out of a leather disc cut out with a ⅜" dia (9.0mm) drive punch tool and a ³⁄₁₆" dia (4.5mm) or ³⁄₃₂" dia (2.4mm) hole (depending on which snap part it is used for).

7 Using a setter and an anvil, rivet the snaps in place. Regulate your force, as too much of it might flatten the snaps too much.

8 We have riveted the snaps. Check that they are well positioned and won't detach.

9 Finish off the edges that you cannot retouch later. If the leather is very thin, just sand them down.

10 The edges that need to be finished are marked in red in the picture.

11 Fold the paper patterns in two vertically, place them on the flesh sides of the leather pieces, and mark the central line with a round awl.

12 Sand down the mark to a ³⁄₁₆" (5mm)-large vertical strip and apply flex glue.

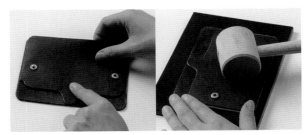

13 Align the leather pieces and glue the two central lines together. Gently press the leather with a wooden mallet. The sides and bottom have yet to be glued together.

14 Trace the first and last stitching points that are on the paper pattern to the leather. Link them with a stitching groove made with a bone folder.

15 With the compass, mark the stitching holes with ¼" (6mm) spacing. The marks should be even and should mirror the paper pattern.

16 Go over these marks with a ³⁄₃₂" dia (2.4mm) drive punch tool. Opening holes with three punch tools welded together makes the task easier.

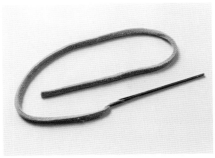

17 Cut a deerskin cord twice the length of the case's height and thread a darning needle.

▶ Running stitch no.1

1 Starting between the two layers of leather, lace the second hole, pulling the needle to the back. Then push it to the front of the card holder through the first hole.

19 Leave about ³⁄₁₆" (5mm) of cord tip between the two layers of leather.

2 Push the needle a second time through the second hole, and then continue with a regular running stitch.

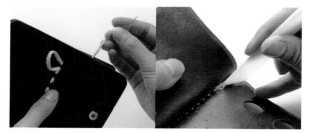

3 When you reach the end, lace the second hole again and push the needle between the layers of leather. Leave a ³⁄₁₆" (5mm) tip. We will glue the tips to the card holder.

4 Apply flex glue to the tips of the cord and the filed inside margin of the card holder. Glue everything together while folding the card holder.

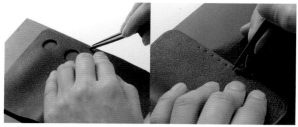

5 Trace a stitching groove around the card holder and then mark the ¼" (6mm)-spaced stitching holes. The number of holes should be even.

6 The first and last holes will only be on the Body (outside) piece. Open the holes with a drive punch tool.

7 Finish off the edges before stitching them together.

▶ Running stitch no.2

1 Starting between the two layers of leather, pull the needle to the front of the second hole and then push it through the first hole to the back of the card holder. Lace the second hole a second time.

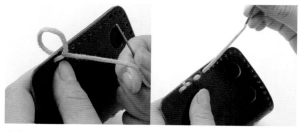

2 Lace the second hole as shown (left) and then continue with a normal running stitch. This is done to strengthen the card holder.

3 After double-stitching the second-to-last hole, lace another time as shown, pulling the needle between the layers of leather. Cut the cord, leaving a ³⁄₈" (5mm) end.

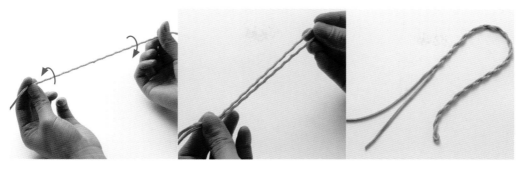

4 To create the strap of the card holder, simply twist a three-foot-long (90cm) deerskin lace and fold it in two. The lace should twist on itself.

5 Tie the ends together with a knot. Leave 6" (15cm) of loose ends.

6 Open a ¾6" dia (4.5mm) hole as in the picture, and thread it with the twisted lace. The loose ends should come out in the front, and the knot on the inside of the fold.

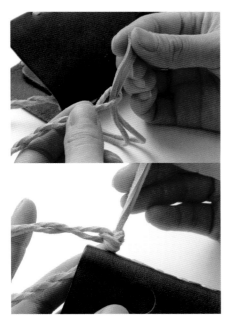

7 Thread the last loop of cord with the loose ends and tie them together with a knot.

To change the look of the card holder, you can use a key ring or other accessory instead of the strap. Have fun arranging it!

Done!

Tote Bag
stitched with a sewing machine

With many long, straight lines to stitch, this is the perfect item to start practicing machine-sewing leather. To make it even easier, we have divided the parts to be sewed into small sections. Of course, you can always decide to hand-sew everything, but it will take considerably more time. The handles will be folded in three to give it more strength, and then sewn by hand.

Hint

In our tutorial, we are using chrome-dyed leather, but you can decide to use vegetable-tanned leather, which would create a more rigid and perhaps elegant-looking bag. You can also change the paper pattern to suit your taste and needs.

WHAT YOU'LL NEED
- Silver pen—Necessary to mark chrome leather.
- You will also need a sewing machine that can be used with leather.

LEATHER USED
- Chromium-tanned cowhide ⅟₃₂" (1.0mm) thick

Crafter: Ikkei Kobayashi

▶ Leather cutting

1 When cutting the body of the tote bag, the handles should be made out of two pieces of 3" x 20" (8 x 50cm) leather, but the length can be altered to suit your tastes.

2 Placing the pattern on the leather, mark with the pen where the handles will be sewn.

3 Do the same with the areas where the leather will be folded back.

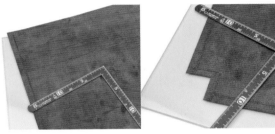

4 With a ruler or a square, trace the seams, $\frac{13}{32}$" (1cm) from the margins. Trace another line to join the points done in Step 3, which will mark where the bag will be folded back.

5 Trace a line 1 $\frac{3}{16}$" (3cm) from the top and 2" (5cm) from the bottom on both handles.

6 We will now open the four slits for the handles. With a $\frac{1}{8}$" dia (3.0mm) drive punch tool, make holes where you marked them.

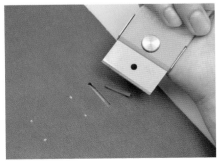

7 Cut between the two holes to make a slit.

8 Don't cut further than the hole. To end your cut, try to cut it in reverse, as shown.

▶ Sewing

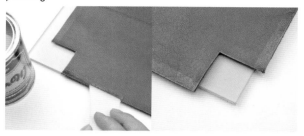

1 Apply some rubber cement adhesive to the sewing strip. This adhesive is used temporarily, so there is no need to abrade the strip.

2 Once the glue is dry, stick the body of the bag together. Carefully align the corners together.

3 Stitch with the sewing machine along the line you previously traced. You can do it by hand, but given the amount of stitches it might be a little tedious.

4 Once sewn, slightly burn the end of the thread.

5 Open the seamed margin you had glued together. Take care not to damage the leather.

6 Rub the glue until it forms a ball and peel it off.

7 Apply flex glue on a ³⁄₃₂" (2cm) margin for each side of the seams, but, like in the picture, leave out the corners.

8 Now fold over the margins at the base of the seam and glue them together.

138

9 Flatten well with a roller.

10 Having seamed three sides of the leather pieces, this is how your work should look.

11 Apply rubber cement to the seams of the inside of the corners (the grain side) and close the corners together.

12 Glue well by gently hammering them with a wooden mallet.

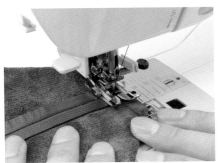

13 Stitch the traced seam.

14 Once the two corners have been closed, your bag should have a square bottom to it.

15 Apply rubber cement all over the area where the leather will be folded back, but leave out the area where the handles will be placed.

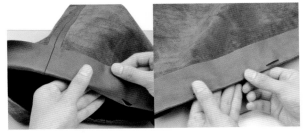

16 Fold the glued leather in two, taking care not to create any wrinkles.

17 When you fold over the leather, make sure that the seams are all aligned.

18 Flatten the glued leather with a roller and the sides of the wooden mallet.

19 This is how your tote should now look.

20 Turn your bag inside out.

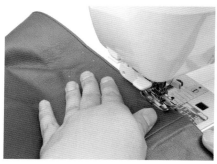

21 With the sewing machine, make a seam ⅛" (3mm) away from the edges.

22 Take extra care not to sew in the slits for the bag handles.

▶ Creating the handles

1 We will fold the handles in three. First, apply gum to the 2" (5cm) strip and fold that over in two.

2 Pass the roller over the strip.

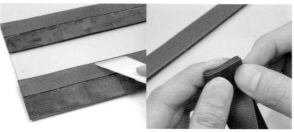

3 Now, apply gum on both 1 ³⁄₁₆" (3cm) strips and the folded-over leather. Fold that together.

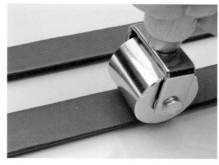

4 Remove any creases or wrinkles with the roller.

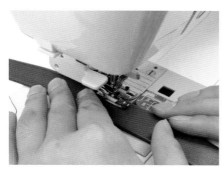

5 Sew the leather together by stitching a seam ⅛" (3mm) from the margins.

Once you have sewn them into strips, you can attach them to the bag.

▶ Sewing the handles and finishing off the bag

1 Insert the handles through the slits you created beforehand.

2 Insert it until you have reached the end of the folded-over leather. Don't twist the straps.

3 Apply rubber cement between the straps and the body of the bag.

4 This is how the handles should be, in relation to the bag body.

5 Before hand sewing, open the four cardinal points with a round awl and link them with your silver pen. They should form an X.

6 Open the stitching slits with a thonging chisel.

7 Start sewing the leather with two needles. The first and last stitch should be backstitched.

8 The last stitch should come out on the inside of the bag. As the thread is synthetic, you can melt their tips to seal the seams.

9 This is how it should look.

Done!

10 Do the same with the remaining three handles' ends.

Once you have learned the basics, you can easily change the size of this smart bag to suit your needs.

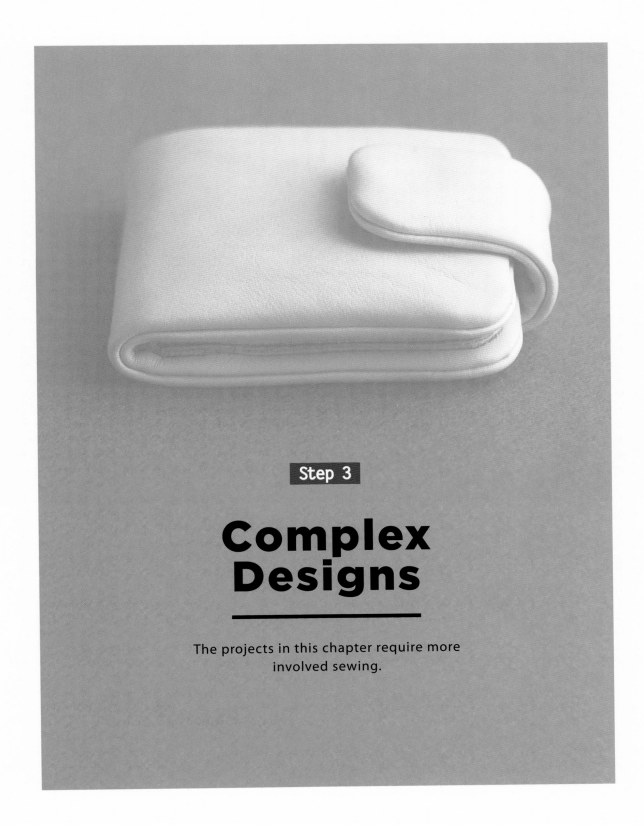

Complex Designs

The projects in this chapter require more involved sewing.

Sewing multiple layers of leather together for a
Medium-Sized Wallet

This is a highly spacious classic bifold wallet. You can slip in your bills, store your cards vertically, and also carry your coins in a small inside pocket. But its sleek and simple design makes it a very slim wallet to carry on you.

Hint

By stitching the inner fold of the wallet together, the bill compartment will automatically open with your wallet. Here, we used ⅛" (2.5mm)-thick vegetable-tanned leather to give the wallet a sturdy look.

Crafter: Ikkei Kobayashi
▶ Paper pattern pages 168–169

WHAT YOU'LL NEED
- A diamond-shaped awl. This tool is often used to pierce thicker leather and can be used without any support.
- Zip—We will use a 6" (16cm) zip.
- Screw-on ring or ring stud—This is a ring on a ball stud with a screwed end. To prevent it from unscrewing, just apply some flex gluein between.

LEATHER USED
- Body: Saddle leather ⅛" (2.5mm) thick
- Inner: Saddle leather 1/16" (1.5mm) thick
- Card pocket: 1/32" (1.2mm) thick

▶ Cutting the pieces and other preparations

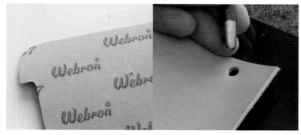

1 Cut out the pieces of leather according to the paper pattern. In the case of the corner that is a curve, a drive punch is used.

2 The hole in the center is opened with a ½" dia (12mm) drive punch tool and a ³⁄₁₆" dia (4.5mm) for the side holes.

3 Link the two ³⁄₁₆" dia (4.5mm) holes by following the pattern, and you will get an elegant design.

4 Apply glossing polish on all the flesh sides and rub until it shines.

5 The edges marked with red need to be finished off now.

6 Finish them by beveling them, sanding them down, and applying polish. The hole can be finished with heavy canvas.

▶ Creating the coin pocket

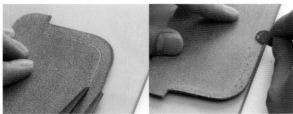

1 On the coin pocket pieces, trace guidelines that will help you glue the zipper on. These should be ⁵⁄₁₆" (8mm) from the edge and should be sanded down as shown.

2 Apply flex glue on both the sanded-down leather and the zipper's tape—⁹⁄₃₂" (7mm) margin.

3 Start by sticking the straight leather edge with the tape. We will do the angle after this is done.

4 Glue the curved part by creating folds like in the picture.

5 Glue the zipper's tape on the other piece of leather and then check that there are no creases when you close the zipper.

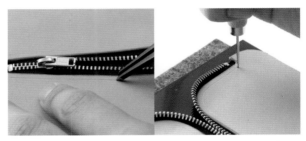

6 Now create a stitching groove ⅛" (3mm) from the edges. Open the reference points with the round awl.

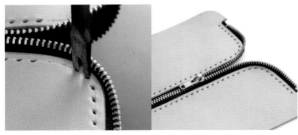

7 Open the stitching slits with a thonging chisel, and use the two-pronged one to do the curved corner.

8 Proceed by stitching the zipper to the coin pocket with two needles.

9 With flex glue, glue the tape ends as shown.

10 Double-check that the zipper closes well.

▶ Creating the card holder

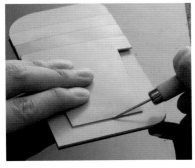

1 Put the card holder pieces together and mark where they should be sewn.

2 Sand down the portions that have to be sewn together. We show these in red in the picture.

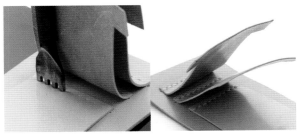

3 Apply flex glue and open the stitching slits. The holes that pierce the base should only be opened with a round awl and not a thonging chisel.

4 Apply flex glue on both the "sleeves" of the T-shaped pieces and the three lower margins of your last card holder piece.

5 As usual, sand the edges down.

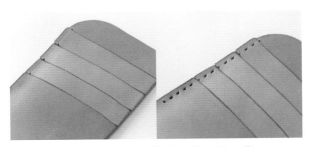

6 We'll start stitching the left side. Open the slits on the edges with a round awl, and the rest with a thonging chisel.

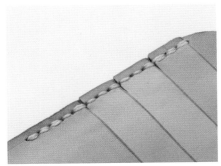

7 The stitches on the edges should be sewn twice to make them stronger.

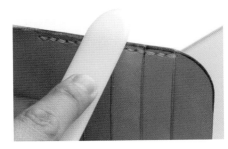

8 Finish off the edges as usual.

 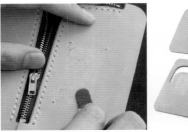 

9 Place both the back of the card holder and the coin pocket on the body of the wallet. Mark the four angles that will be sewn together. Link those points with a round awl, and you should end up with four frames.

10 Sand down the inside of these four frames and apply flex glue.

11 Glue the back of the card holder and the coin pocket on the wallet and trace the stitching grooves.

12 Open the slits with a thonging chisel and sew everything together.

13 Note where the coin pocket and back of the card holder will have to be sewn, and sand these edges down. Apply flex glue.

14 Once you've glued the coin pocket and the back of the card holder with the card holder itself, sand down the edges.

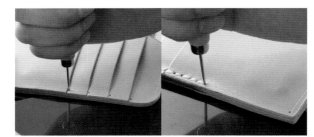 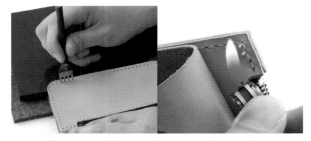

15 Create the stitching grooves and, just like in the picture, open the cardinal points with a round awl and do the rest of the stitching slits with a thonging chisel. Sew everything.

16 Do the same with the coin pocket. Once you've sewn that up too, pull the threads to the back and seal them with a flame.

▶ Putting the last pieces together

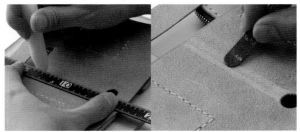

1 Turn the wallet upside down and sand down a ¹³⁄₃₂" (1cm) strip in the middle—³⁄₁₆" (5mm) on both sides of the fold.

2 Wet the bone folder with water and make a crease in the middle. Fold the wallet in two and make the crease sharper with the side of the wooden mallet.

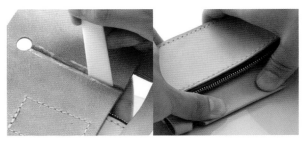

3 Apply flex glue on the sanded-down strip and glue the fold as shown.

4 While the glue is drying, start beveling the edges of the cover, create the groove along which you will sew, and open the stitching slits with a thonging chisel.

5 Open the slits once the glue is dry. The very first and last slits should go on the side of the leather and not on the leather. See the picture.

6 The first and last three stitches should be backstitched (sewn twice) and laced on the side as shown.

7 By stitching the middle, your wallet will automatically open its bill compartment when you unfold it.

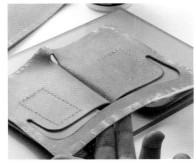

8 To glue the inside with its cover, apply a ³⁄₁₆" (5mm) strip of flex glue on the edges of both pieces.

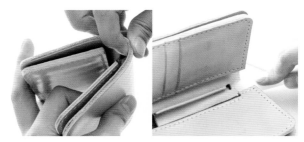

9 Bend the leather when gluing the fold itself, and as you do it, make sure that the edges are aligned with each other. Glue tightly.

10 Once the glue is dry, sand down the edges.

11 Trace a stitching groove on the reverse side. It should roughly be the same as the cover's.

12 Go over the slits you opened in Step 4 until you pierce the other side of the cover.

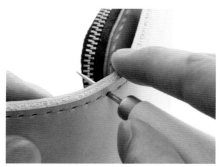

13 To pierce the curve, pierce the slits with the diamond awl. Your holes should come out straight if you aim at the stitching groove traced in Step 11.

14 Stitch the last part of your wallet. Backstitch the first and last few holes and then flatten the stitches with a bone folder.

15 You will now have finished assembling your wallet.

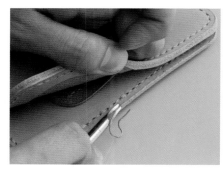

16 Now, to finish the edges, bevel them.

17 Then, with a sanding stick, make the edges smooth and rounder.

18 With a cotton swab, carefully apply glossing polish on the edges. Don't spill it anywhere else!

19 Rub with a bone folder.

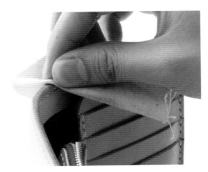

20 Finish burnishing with a heavy canvas.

21 Lastly, cut out a hole with a ⅛" dia (3.0mm) drive punch tool, ¹³⁄₃₂" (1cm) from the edge. Screw on the ring stud with a little flex glue.

Done!

Congratulations! You have just created your own wallet.

Babouches

sewn with cross-stitches and double-loop stitches

These slippers are made from four pieces of leather stitched together. They are comfortable, and as they are made out of leather, they are also extremely breathable. A cushion has also been added between the sole and the insole to make them snug.

Hint

We will use pliable and resistant leather to preserve the shape of the shoe. We recommend using vegetable-tanned leather that has been softened and crumpled beforehand. You can sew these shoes either with your sewing machine or by hand, and of course change the colors to suit your tastes!

Crafter: Megumi Hoshi

WHAT YOU'LL NEED
- Contact cement—The pliability after completion is secured, and in order to weaken resistance at the time of letting a lace pass in a hole, the natural rubber cement for temporary stops is used.
- Tools for lacing leather

LEATHER USED
- Upper: Shrinking cowhide ³⁄₃₂" (2.3mm) thick
- Heel: Shrinking cowhide ¹⁄₁₆" (1.7mm) thick
- Insole: Pig suede
- Sole: Split ³⁄₃₂" (2mm) thick
- Cushion: Felt ¼" (6mm) thick

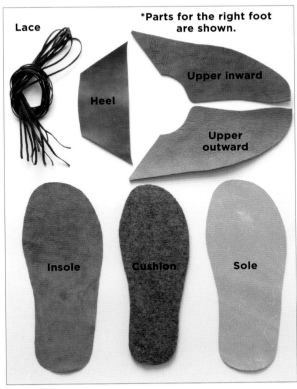

Lace

Parts for the right foot are shown.

Upper inward

Heel

Upper outward

Insole   Cushion   Sole

1 You will need about 36" (90cm) of ⅛" (3mm)-wide cowhide lace. For smaller slippers, cut it out in 16 strings, and in 20 for bigger ones.

2 It is important that you now trace all the marks from the patterns onto the leather. You won't be able to do this later.

3 Finish off the edges you won't be able to retouch later.

4 Stick the upper parts together by applying glue on a ⅛" (3mm)-wide margin. The strip should go from one mark to the other.

5 Create a stitching groove on both the edges that you have just glued and on the edges that will be sewn to the sole.

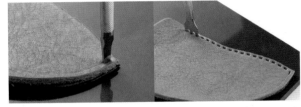

6 The slit closest to the tip of the shoes has to be opened on the sole's stitching groove. The rest can be opened on the central groove.

▶ The cross-stitch

1 Push the needle between the layers and into the slit on the sole's stitching groove. Pass the needle through the second slit by inserting it from the same side as your first stitch.

2 Pass the needle through the third slit, always from the same side. Continue to do this up to the last slit, and you will get a spiral of lace around the edge of the upper.

3 This type of sewing is called the whipstitch. To get a cross-stitch, we need to backstitch the whole seam from the other side to get a lot of "x" stitches. Make the holes bigger with the lacing needle.

4 Once you've reached the tip of the slipper, insert the needle through the slit opposite your first stitch.

5 The two ends of the lace should come out on the grain side. Cut them ¹³⁄₃₂" (1cm) from their base, flatten them, and glue them with contact cement.

6 Spread out the upper, and with the handle of the wooden mallet open up the base of the seam to give the slipper some shape.

7 To sew the uppers to the heel, glue the marked margins of the heel over the upper parts. Give it some pinch with the hammer.

8 Create a stitching groove ⅛" (3mm) from the border on the heel.

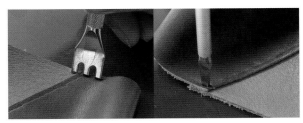

9 Just like with the uppers, the lowest slit will have to be pierced on the sole's stitching groove. With a three-pronged chisel, mark where the slit (the middle prong) should go by placing it like in the left-hand picture, then pierce it with a one-pronged chisel (above right).

10 Open the other slits as usual.

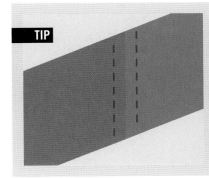

11 Open more slits on the edges of the upper, parallel and aligned with the slits on the heel. See the diagram, right.

TIP

If you put the stitching groove vertically, you can see that the slits are aligned with each other, save for one slit's difference. When lacing, though, lace as shown, linking the first slit on one side to the first slit on the other, and so on.

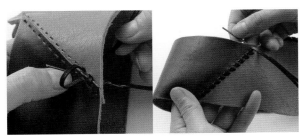

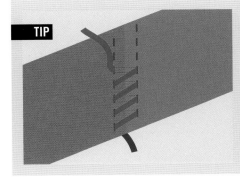

12 We won't use the slit made on the sole's groove. Start with the lowest perpendicular slit and push the lace from behind. Continue the whipstitch until you reach the top.

TIP

This shows you how the whipstitch should be laced.

13 When you've stitched your last slit, bring the lace to the front, push the needle through the second slit, and continue to whipstitch in the opposite direction.

TIP

By continuing to sew in this manner you will get a cross-stitched seam.

14 When you sew your last stitch, the lace should come out from behind. Cut the ends and glue them with contact cement.

15 Sew the other seam, and the upper part is finished.

16 Apply glue on one side of the sole cushion and glue it to the flesh side of the sole. As you can see, the cushion is smaller than the sole, so glue it in the middle of the sole.

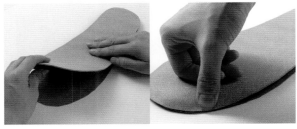

17 Glue the two pieces to the insole, aligning the edges of the insole to the sole's. Press the borders well.

18 Make sure that there are no gaps by going over the borders with the handle of your mallet. You should be able to see the shape of the cushion.

19 We will glue the lower part of the slipper to the upper part. Start by aligning all the marks you copied from the paper pattern, and glue.

20 Stick the leather evenly, and make sure there are no creases or wrinkles. Once you've done that, mark a stitching groove ⅛" (3mm) from the edge.

21 Pierce the three slits that you opened beforehand until it pierces the sole. Don't damage the leather lace.

22 From these three holes, open the other slits in the usual way. Be careful, as it can be tricky to align them well.

23 To be able to seal your lace ends in a discreet way, start your double-loop stitch from the middle of a side.

▶ Double-loop stitch

1 Double-loop lacing is a beautifully textured stitch. Follow the instructions on page 32 and stitch all around.

2 Push the tip of your babouche outward as shown. This will give it a nicer form.

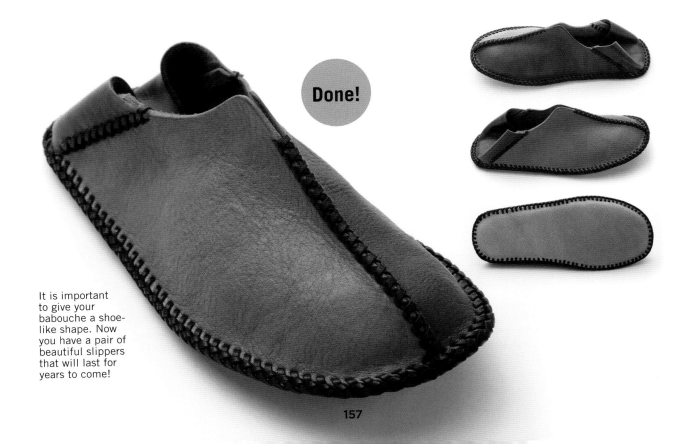

Done!

It is important to give your babouche a shoe-like shape. Now you have a pair of beautiful slippers that will last for years to come!

Bifold Wallet

with machine-sewn invisible seams

We have created a wallet with invisible seams that could be folded in two. By inserting foam in the linings, we get it to puff up a little for a cuter look. It is compact and has a lot of inside pockets, and thanks to its flap closure, it can easily be carried in a bag without losing anything.

Hint

Although it can be sewn by hand, these invisible seams were designed specifically for the more discreet machine-sewn stitches. To get this puffed-up look, use elastic and light leather. Sewing by machine will be easier if you glue the stitching lines together with a hammer.

Crafter: Megumi Hoshi

WHAT YOU'LL NEED
- Rubber cement—The needle might get stuck if you use a strong adhesive. We will avoid this problem with a weaker adhesive.
- Silver pen—On soft leather, it's easier to see marks done with a silver pen than a round awl. But you can only use it for the linings, because it cannot be rubbed out.
- Standard iron hammer—With a firmer head than the wooden mallet, it will make neat folds and iron out seams. A standard hammer will do the job.
- A sewing machine is required.

LEATHER USED
- Chrome-tanned cowhide
- Lining cloth of cotton
- Sponge with paste ⅛" (3mm) thick

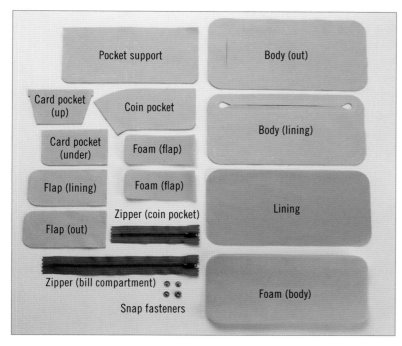

Snap fasteners

1 Cut out the leather. The two foam flaps will have to be ⅛" (3mm) thick, making it ¼" (6mm) when put together. The coin pocket's zipper should be 3" (7.5cm) long, and the bill compartment's zipper 8" (20cm) long. Get medium-sized snap fasteners and replace the snap cap with a flat post. If you think you need padding between the snaps and the leather, have some ready. A size 14 (9.0mm) drive punch tool is used.

2 The cut in the Body (lining) should be created with one straight cut with holes at both ends opened with a ¹³⁄₃₂" dia (10.5mm) drive punch tool. Make the holes teardrop-shaped as shown.

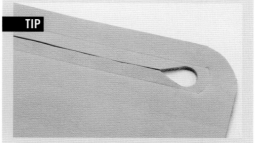

TIP

Mark the stitching groove for the zipper with a round awl and not the silver pen.

▶ Creating the card pockets

1 Sew simple running stitches on the top parts of the two Card pocket pieces.

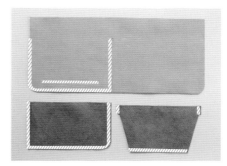

2 The marks show where the seams will go. Apply gum glue to them.

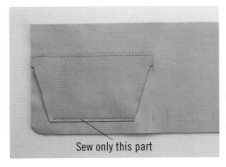

Sew only this part

3 Glue the first Card pocket on the Pocket support. Sew the bottom only.

Make the seam L-shaped

4 Glue the second Card pocket in line with the first one, and sew the right edge top-down, sewing ⅟₃₂" (1cm) more past the corner.

▶ Creating the coin pocket

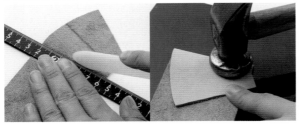

1 Mark the folds of the pocket before you sew it. Start by tracing them on the flesh side with a bone folder and then finish the folds with your hammer.

2 Create a gusset by stitching the first fold together.

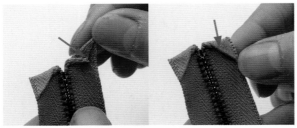

3 Fold the edges of the tape to the back twice like in the picture.

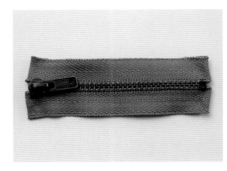

4 The front of the zipper should look like this now. The zipper should be 3" (7.5cm) long.

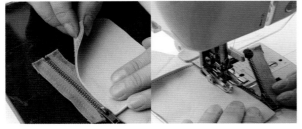

5 Glue the top of the coin pocket to the lower tape of the zipper with the gum glue, and sew them together. Refer to the patterns to make sure they are sewn in the correct position.

6 If you are left-handed, stitch the zipper in the opposite direction.

7 Stitch the other tape to the Pocket support. Make sure the two pieces of leather fit together.

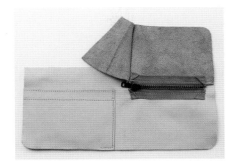

8 Your wallet should look like this at this point.

9 Glue the right and bottom edges together. Glue the lower edge of the gusset too.

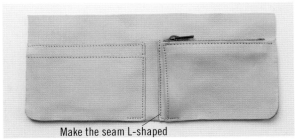

Make the seam L-shaped

10 Sew the left edges in the same manner of the Card pockets, and when sewing the corner, sew the folded gusset too.

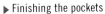

▶ Finishing the pockets

1 Apply a 1³⁄₁₆" (3cm) strip of gum glue on the reverse upper edge of the Pocket support. Fold that strip in two, and you should get a ¹⁹⁄₃₂" (1.5cm) folded strip.

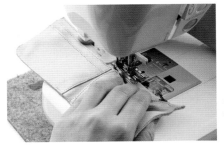

2 Sew the edge of the fold you have just made.

3 The coin pockets and the card holders are now finished. You can iron out all the folds with the hammer.

▶ Sewing the zipper to the Body (lining)

1 When stitching the zipper to the leather, take care not to be out of alignment with the cut in the leather. Apply the rubber cement to the highlighted parts.

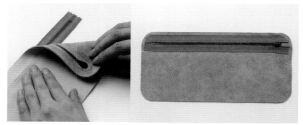

2 Glue the zipper to the leather by aligning it with the slit. Cut any excess tape.

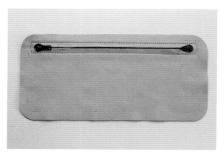

3 Machine-sew the zipper to the leather by following the stitching line traced with the round awl.

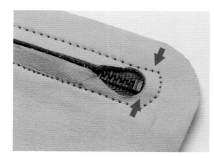

4 Be particularly careful when sewing close to the teardrop-shaped opening, because there is very little space between the stitching line and the hole.

▶ Sewing the pockets and finishing the inside part of the wallet

1 Glue the pockets to the Body (lining) by aligning it with the marks done on the Body. You will need to fold the center fold of the Body slightly in order to do this. Sew the sides of the pocket with two L-shaped seams that go from the top-external corners to the low-inside corners.

2 You should not stitch the middle, so stop sewing when you reach the lowest inside corners.

▶ Stitching the flap

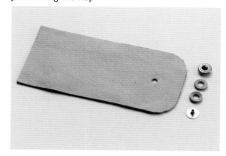

1 Using a ³⁄₁₆" dia drive punch tool (4.5mm), open a hole in the flap (lining) to attach the snaps. Prepare a few pads to place between the snaps and the flap.

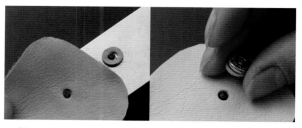

2 Place a pad between the grain side and the socket of the snap fasteners. Place another one between the flesh side and the flat post. Make sure the pads are made of sturdy leather to prevent the snaps from flattening.

3 Cut out a leather disc and glue it with rubber cement to the flat post. Just apply some glue on the flat post. This will make the flap look smoother.

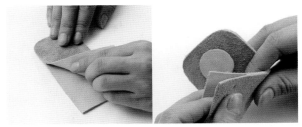

4 Glue the flaps together grain side on grain side by applying a ⅛" (3mm) margin of gum glue on both sides. Leave the bottom unglued.

5 Machine-sew these three glued edges.

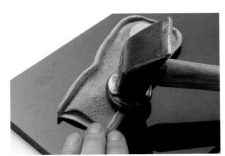

6 To make it easier to reverse the flap, fold the edges with the hammer.

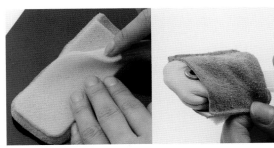

7 Glue the foam on both sides of the flap and turn the flap inside out using a bone folder.

8 Make the folds neater with the hammer.

9 Apply rubber cement inside the unsewn edges and stick them together while folding the flap.

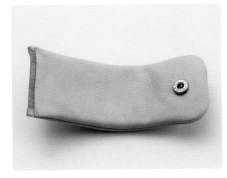

10 The bottom of the flap should be misaligned, just like in the picture. The shorter side is the inside of the flap.

▶ Stitching the outer part of the body

1 Insert the flap in the cut of the Body (out), double-checking that it is done in the right way. Glue the flesh side first and then the grain side.

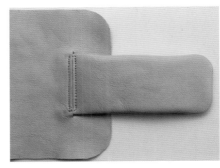

2 Sew all around the slit as if you were stitching a very thin rectangle. Flatten the stitches well with the hammer.

3 Open the hole on the Body (out) with a ³⁄₃₂" dia (2.4mm) drive punch tool. Fix the eyelet and stud to it.

4 Glue the foam on the flesh side in the center of the Body (out). The foam should be smaller than the piece of leather.

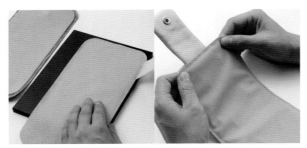

5 Applying glue on the edges of the Lining, stick the Lining to the Body (out). Don't glue the foam.

6 Now that we have sandwiched the foam between the Lining and the outer part of the wallet, we will start finishing it off.

▶ Finishing off the wallet

1 Apply rubber cement to the entire contour of the grain sides of the two pieces. Take care not to glue the flap too.

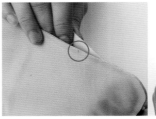

2 As the inside part is smaller than the outside part, align the two marks together and start gluing them while bending the wallet. You should then be able to glue the two pieces together in alignment with each other.

3 Sew the edges together, starting from a bottom corner.

4 Leave the zipper open, as you will turn the wallet inside out from there.

5 Fold the edges and neaten them with the hammer, just like we did in Step 31. You can then turn the wallet inside out.

6 Finish by flattening the edges with the hammer.

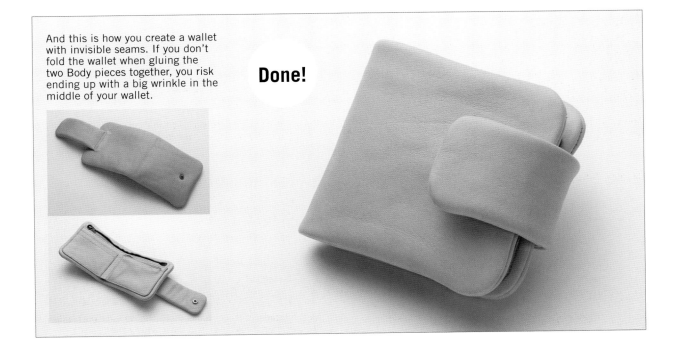

And this is how you create a wallet with invisible seams. If you don't fold the wallet when gluing the two Body pieces together, you risk ending up with a big wrinkle in the middle of your wallet.

Done!

FULL-SIZE PAPER PATTERNS

Copy them onto thicker paper or use a thin paper and then glue it to cardboard. It is important to be as precise as possible in making the patterns. You will also be able to use these patterns multiple times.

*Measurements with "dia" (diameter) indicate the size of the drive punch tool to be used. First, mark the position of the hole with a round awl, and then punch it open.
*The sewing marks are first lightly pricked with a round awl and then fully opened just before stitching.

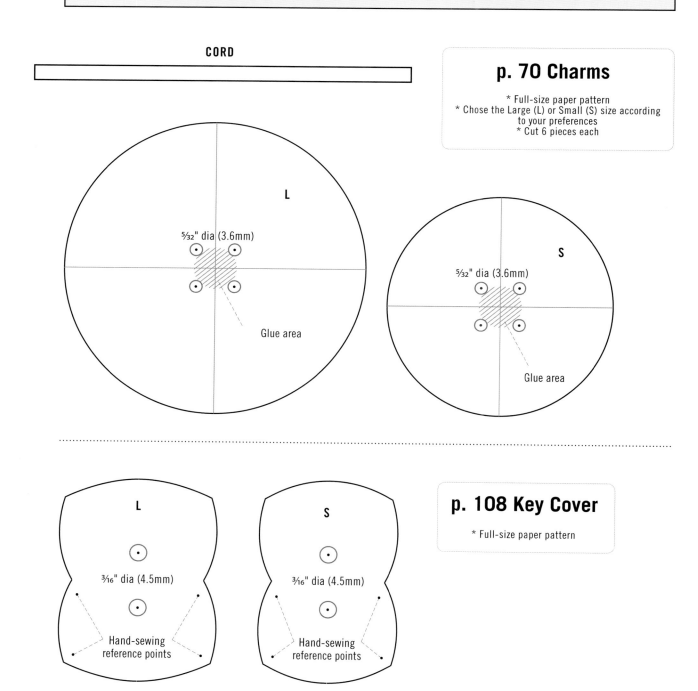

CORD

p. 70 Charms

* Full-size paper pattern
* Chose the Large (L) or Small (S) size according to your preferences
* Cut 6 pieces each

L

5⁄32" dia (3.6mm)

Glue area

S

5⁄32" dia (3.6mm)

Glue area

p. 108 Key Cover

* Full-size paper pattern

L

3⁄16" dia (4.5mm)

Hand-sewing reference points

S

3⁄16" dia (4.5mm)

Hand-sewing reference points

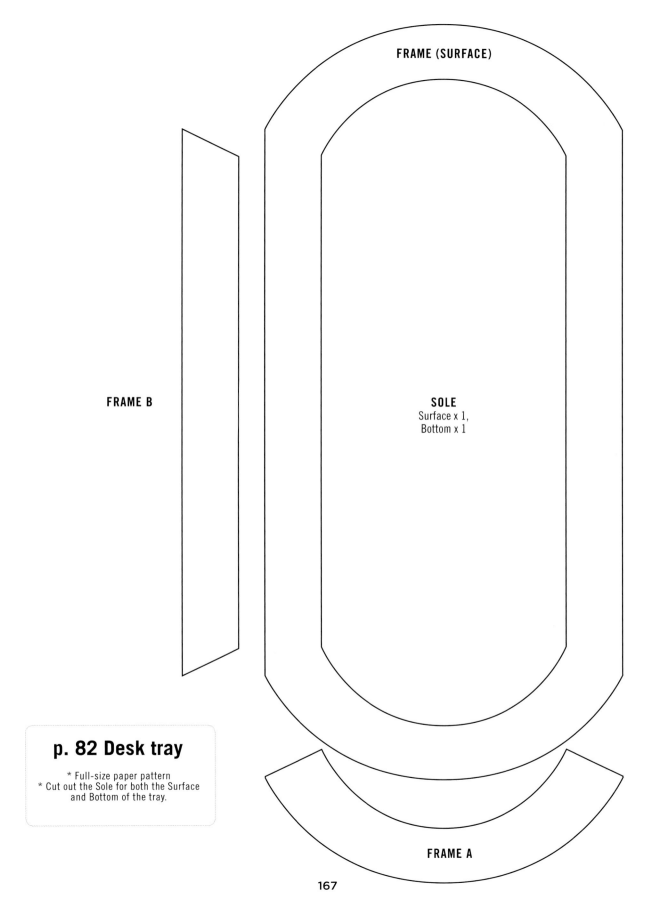

FRAME (SURFACE)

FRAME B

SOLE
Surface x 1,
Bottom x 1

p. 82 Desk tray

* Full-size paper pattern
* Cut out the Sole for both the Surface
and Bottom of the tray.

FRAME A

p. 144 Medium-Sized Wallet

* Full-size paper pattern
* Cut out the Main Body and open a size 2 (3.0mm) hole
* Use both sides of the pattern to cut out the two pieces of the card holder and the coin pocket

MAIN BODY (LINING)

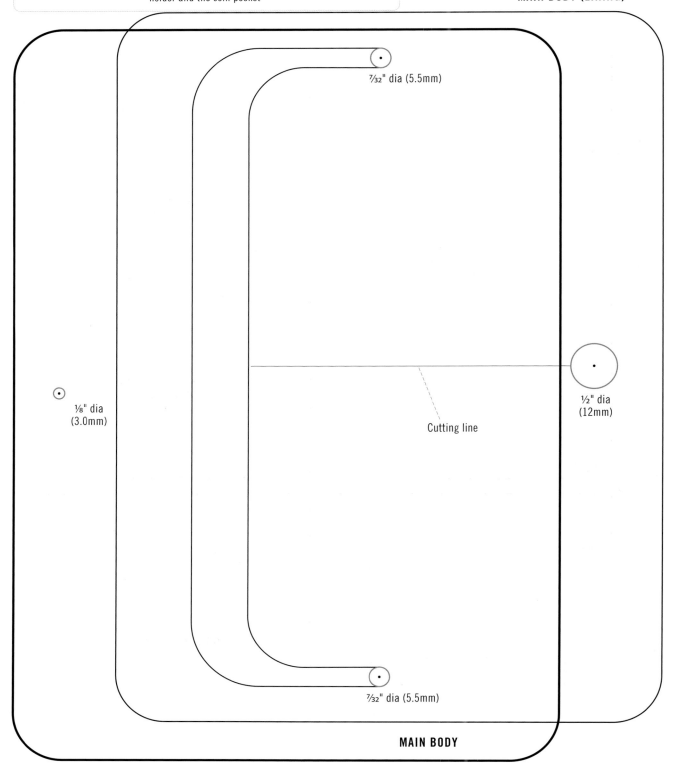

7/32" dia (5.5mm)

1/8" dia (3.0mm)

1/2" dia (12mm)

Cutting line

7/32" dia (5.5mm)

MAIN BODY

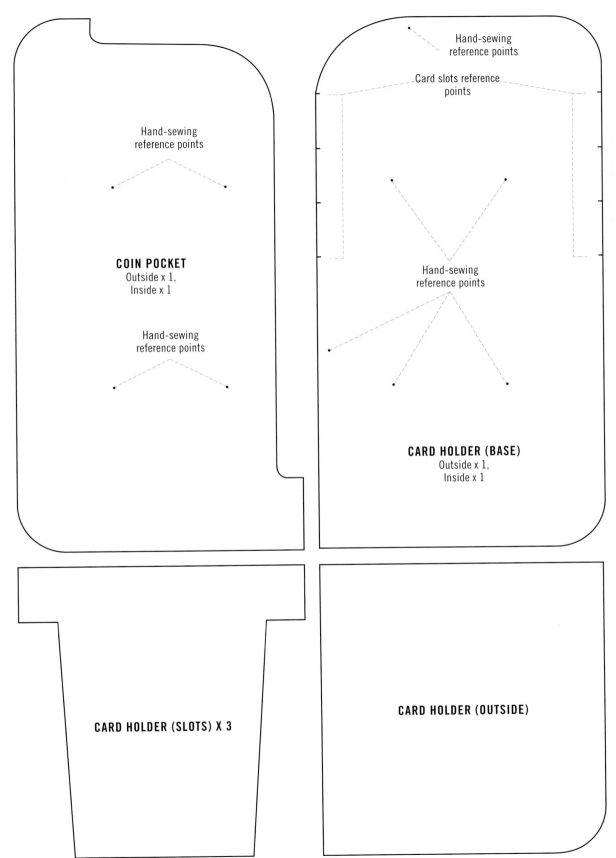

Hand-sewing
reference points

Card slots reference
points

Hand-sewing
reference points

COIN POCKET
Outside x 1,
Inside x 1

Hand-sewing
reference points

Hand-sewing
reference points

CARD HOLDER (BASE)
Outside x 1,
Inside x 1

CARD HOLDER (SLOTS) X 3

CARD HOLDER (OUTSIDE)

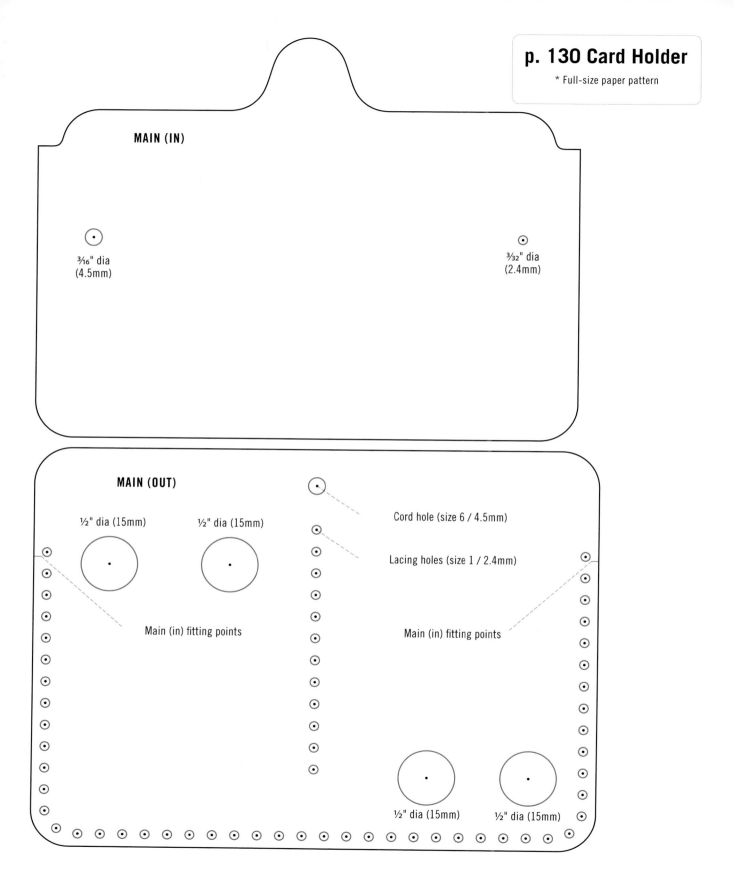

MAIN (IN)

³⁄₁₆" dia (4.5mm)

³⁄₃₂" dia (2.4mm)

MAIN (OUT)

½" dia (15mm)

½" dia (15mm)

Cord hole (size 6 / 4.5mm)

Lacing holes (size 1 / 2.4mm)

Main (in) fitting points

Main (in) fitting points

½" dia (15mm)

½" dia (15mm)

* Full-size paper pattern

p. 112 Pen Cover
* Full-size paper pattern

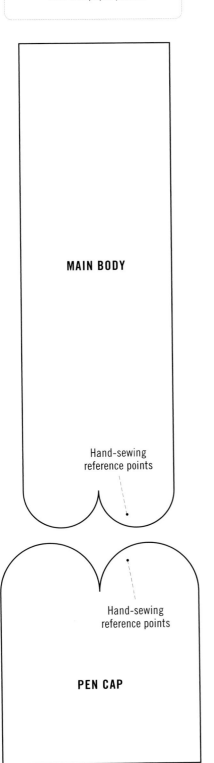

MAIN BODY

Hand-sewing
reference points

Hand-sewing
reference points

PEN CAP

p. 60 Tassels
* Full-size paper pattern

A

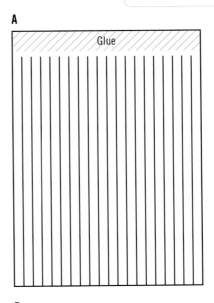

Glue

B

Glue

C
* Check the length of this glue strip when working on it

Glue

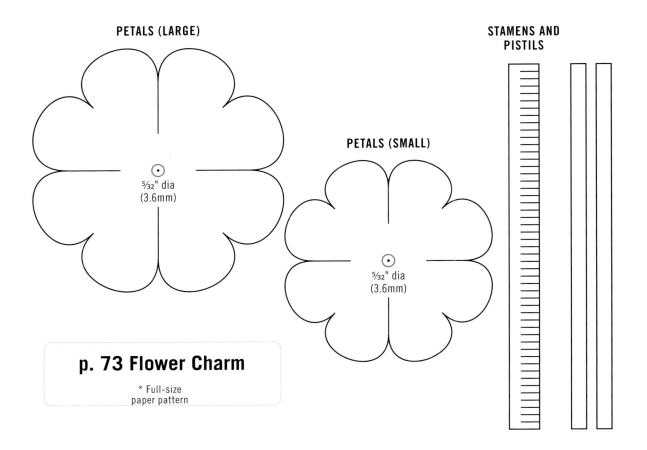

PETALS (LARGE)

PETALS (SMALL)

STAMENS AND PISTILS

⁵⁄₃₂" dia (3.6mm)

⁵⁄₃₂" dia (3.6mm)

p. 73 Flower Charm

* Full-size
paper pattern

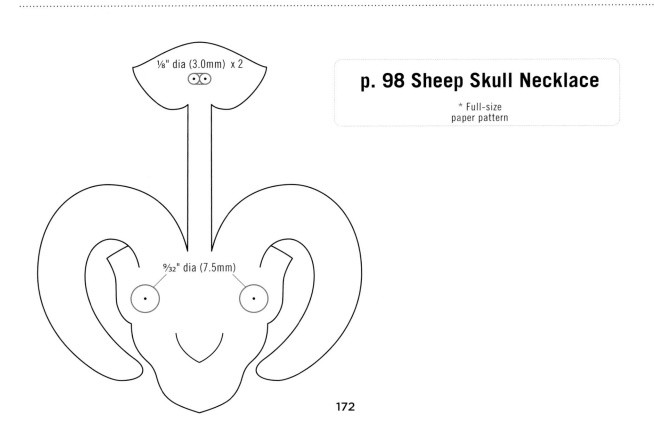

⅛" dia (3.0mm) x 2

p. 98 Sheep Skull Necklace

* Full-size
paper pattern

⁹⁄₃₂" dia (7.5mm)

p. 64 Bracelet

* Full-size paper pattern
* The decorations should be copied onto tracing paper

ENGRAVED BRACELET

⁵⁄₃₂" dia (3.6mm)

¹⁄₁₆" dia (1.8mm)

¹⁄₈" dia (3.0mm)

MEN'S

³⁄₁₆" dia (4.5mm)

¹⁄₁₆" dia (1.8mm)

¹⁄₈" dia (3.0mm)

Ladies'

³⁄₁₆" dia (4.5mm)

¹⁄₁₆" dia (1.8mm)

¹⁄₈" dia (3.0mm)

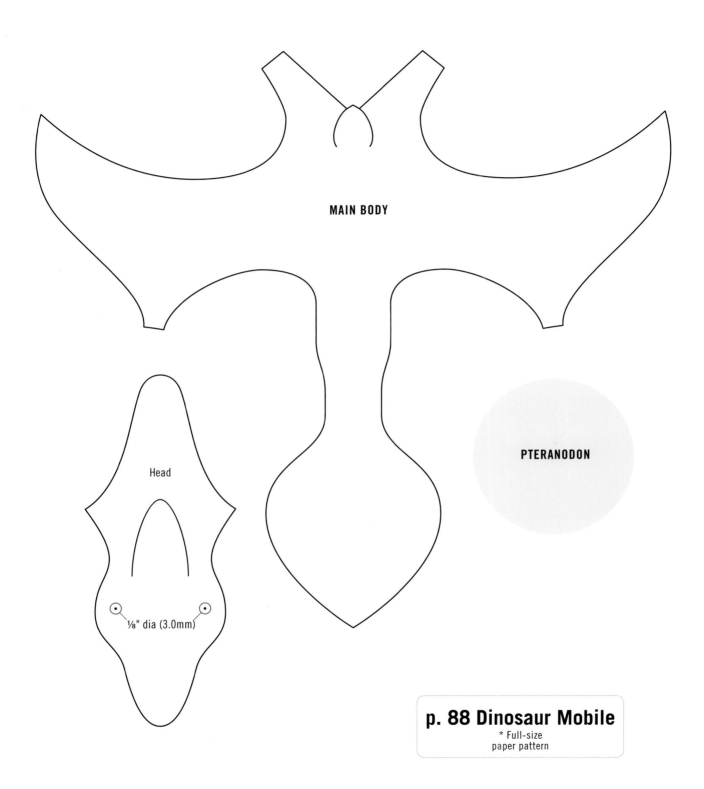

MAIN BODY

PTERANODON

Head

⅛" dia (3.0mm)

p. 88 Dinosaur Mobile
* Full-size
paper pattern

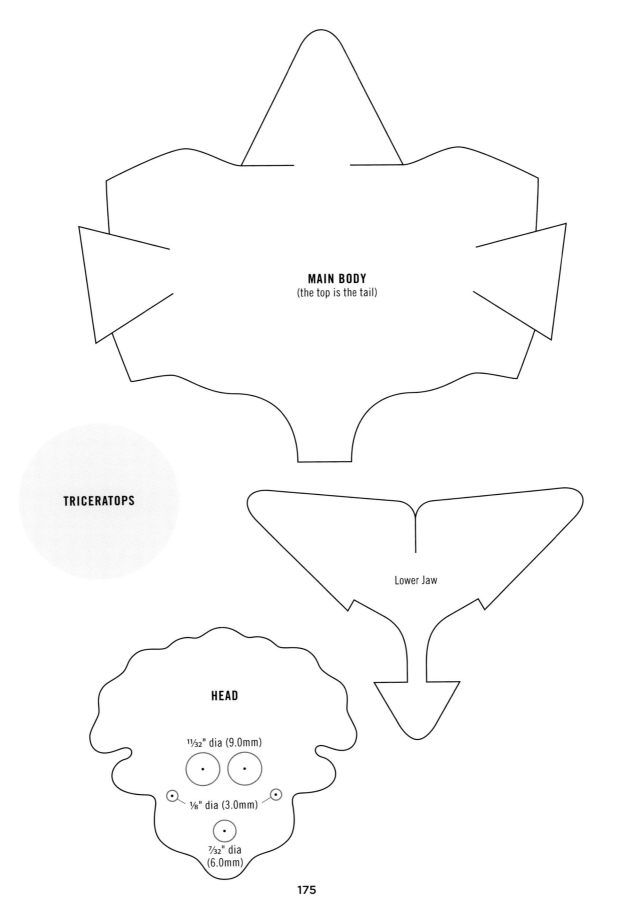

MAIN BODY
(the top is the tail)

TRICERATOPS

Lower Jaw

HEAD

11/32" dia (9.0mm)

1/8" dia (3.0mm)

7/32" dia
(6.0mm)

Index